LOVE CAM

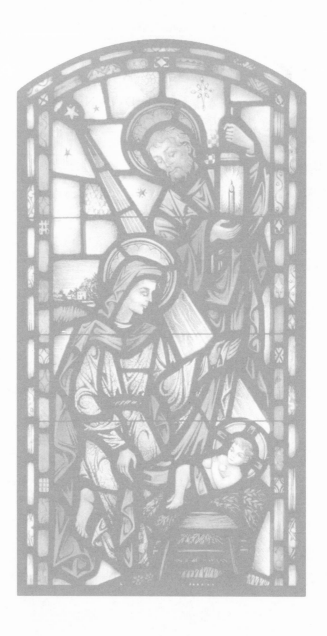

Love Came Down

Anglican Readings
for Advent and Christmas

COMPILED BY

Christopher L. Webber

ABC Publishing
ANGLICAN BOOK CENTRE
TORONTO ■ CANADA

MOREHOUSE PUBLISHING
HARRISBURG, PENNSYLVANIA

ACKNOWLEDGMENTS

I am very grateful to John Gatta for assistance in locating material by Harriet Beecher Stowe and Christina Rossetti and to Roger White for assistance with materials by and about R. W. Church.

Copyright © 2002 by Christopher L. Webber

Morehouse Publishing
P.O. Box 1321
Harrisburg, PA 17105

Anglican Book Centre
600 Jarvis Street
Toronto, Ontario, Canada M4Y2J6

Morehouse Publishing is a division of The Morehouse Group.

Excerpt from *The Crown of the Year* by Austin Farrer. Reprinted by permission of A&C Black.

Excerpt from *The Irrational Season* by Madeleine L'Engle. Copyright © 1977 by Crosswicks, Ltd. Reprinted by permission of HarperCollins Publishers, Inc.

Excerpt from *Introductory Papers on Dante* by Dorothy L. Sayers. Reprinted by permission of David Higham Associates Ltd.

Cover design by Brenda Klinger
Cover art: Nativity scene from St. John the Baptist Episcopal Church, Minneapolis, Minnesota

Library of Congress Cataloging-in-Publication Data

Love came down : Anglican readings for Advent and Christmas / compiled by Christopher L. Webber.
     p. cm.
Includes bibliographical references.
   ISBN 0-8192-1898-7 (pbk.)
   1. Anglican Communion—Prayer-books and devotions—English.
2. Advent—Prayer-books and devotions—English. 3. Christmas—Prayer-books and devotions—English. I. Webber, Christopher
   BX5004 .L68 2002
   242'.33—dc21

                                                              2002006260

Printed in the United States of America
01 02 03 04 05 06   6 5 4 3 2 1

Contents

· ·

Christmastide

Love came down at Christmas,
    Love all lovely, Love Divine;
Love was born at Christmas,
    Star and Angels gave the sign.

Worship we the Godhead,
    Love Incarnate, Love Divine;
Worship we our Jesus:
    But wherewith for sacred sign?

Love shall be our token,
    Love be yours and love be mine,
Love to God and all men,
    Love for plea and gift and sign.

Christina Rossetti

Introduction

Everyone loves to celebrate Christmas, but Advent is often over-looked in the crush. When Christians began to celebrate the birth of Jesus in the sixth century, it seemed logical to them to prepare for it with great care, so they observed the four weeks before Christmas as Advent. These early Christians thought of Christ's coming not only in terms of the past, but also in terms of the present and future. Christ came to earth in the past, but Christ comes to us now in prayer and sacrament and human need, and he will come again at the end of the world. Because the Second Coming lies ahead, the church's Advent prayers, hymns, and readings focus on the final judgment and the end of the world.

Many reading this book will be surprised by the dark themes in the liturgy in the days just before Christmas. In our culture, the time before Christmas is a time of celebration, gift-giving, and parties. The sooner the fun can start the better. It's easy to overlook the significance of Advent in the rush of Christmas shopping. Advent requires some deep thought on serious subjects, and it's harder to sell these themes than Christmas presents at the mall. So Christians who take Advent seriously find themselves looking strangely out of step. Around them the party has started, but they are still in a solemn time of preparation, considering "the shortness and uncertainty of human life."

In the Christian tradition, thoughts about the end of the world have been divided into "four last things": death, judgment, hell, and heaven. These are solemn themes, but the solemnity is mixed with a deep joy. Modern science confirms the Christian belief that this world will come to an end, but Christians can look forward with confidence and joy, knowing that the Creator has ordered all things toward a good end, that a new heaven and a new earth are part of that plan, and that in the midst of an uncertain and insecure world, we can trust God.

Advent is a solemn time, but it is a time of hope, a time to look forward with confidence in God, working with him to accomplish his purpose in the world. Advent is also Mary's season. An expectant mother understands the solemn joy of looking forward. With Mary, we can move toward Bethlehem, where God's purpose is to be fulfilled. All of these themes are explored in these readings.

Bear in mind that while Advent is a solemn time, it is far from sad. There is sometimes as much joy in preparing for a celebration— cleaning house, planning menus, shopping, sending invitations—as in the celebration itself. And Advent is rich in symbolism, with its Advent calendars, wreaths, and candles. Children can learn to love Advent for itself, as well as for the excitement of looking ahead.

Christmas, on the other hand, needs no advocate; it is celebrated around the world by people who have never heard the gospel. The joy of giving extends far beyond the church, but can lead people to seek a deeper reason for that joy. Anglicans especially love to celebrate Christmas and to ponder the incarnation. It is the coming of God into a human life, the joining of the physical and the spiritual. It grounds our understanding of the church as Christ's body and of the sacraments as a physical means of grace.

Together, Advent and Christmas have elicited some of the finest prose and poetry of the Christian tradition: words to inspire us, words for us to ponder, words that can enrich our understanding and draw us closer to the mystery at the center of our faith.

Using This Book

It is important to notice that the length of the Advent season varies from year to year. It always begins on a Sunday, while Christmas may fall on any day of the week. Advent may be as many as twenty-eight days, or as few as twenty-two. There are enough readings here for the longest Advent season, and they are dated to begin on November 27, regardless of when the first Sunday in Advent may be. The last weeks of the Pentecost season begin to present us with Advent themes, so there is no conflict between these readings and the assigned Sunday readings of the lectionary.

Try using these readings as meditations. Allow time not only to read the passages, but to think about them and appropriate them. If you read them in the morning, you can recall the words often during the day and ponder them further. At the end of each page there are a few words from each reading to use as a centering thought to come back to later. If you find it most convenient to read the passage in the evening, the key words are there to help you recall the passage the next day.

Since the readings are intended for devotional rather than scholarly use, occasionally the language has been modified slightly to conform to contemporary American usage, and some passages have been shortened. Brief biographies of the authors may be found at the end of the book.

Advent is a time of renewal. Let these readings help you make this new year a time when Christ can guide you to discover deeper riches in your faith.

THE ADVENT JOURNEY
Daily Readings

Almighty God, give us grace that we may cast away the works of darkness, and put upon us the armor of light, now in the time of this mortal life in which thy Son Jesus Christ came to visit us in great humility; that in the last day, when he shall come again in his glorious majesty to judge both the quick and the dead, we may rise to the life immortal; through him who liveth and reigneth with thee and the Holy Ghost, now and for ever. Amen.
—The Advent Collect, Book of Common Prayer

The Advent Collect
(paraphrased as a sonnet)

Almighty Lord and everlasting God,
Come in the silence of our human night
And give us grace that we may cast away
The works of darkness; from eternal day
Now send to us the armor of your light;
In this brief mortal life protect and guard
Your people whom, in great humility,
Our Savior Christ once visited, that when
On that last day in glorious majesty
To judge the quick and dead he comes again,
We, from our earthbound weaknesses may rise,
Rise to immortal life, unending days,
Through him whose life in Trinity supplies
Now and forever your eternal praise.

Christopher L. Webber

NOVEMBER 27

A reading from The Crown of the Year *by Austin Farrer.*

Our journey sets out from God in our creation, and returns to God at the final judgement. As the bird rises from the earth to fly, and must some time return to the earth from which it rose; so God sends us forth to fly, and we must fall back into the hands of God at last. But God does not wait for the failure of our power and the expiry of our days to drop us back into his lap. He goes himself to meet us and everywhere confronts us. Where is the countenance which we must finally look in the eyes, and not be able to turn away our head? It smiles up at Mary from the cradle, it calls Peter from the nets, it looks on him with grief when he has denied his master. Our judge meets us at every step of our way, with forgiveness on his lips and succor in his hands. He offers us these things while there is yet time. Every day opportunity shortens, our scope for learning our Redeemer's love is narrowed by twenty-four hours, and we come nearer to the end of our journey, when we shall fall into the hands of the living God, and touch the heart of the devouring fire.

Advent brings Christmas, judgement runs out into mercy. For the God who saves us and the God who judges us is one God. We are not, even, condemned by his severity and redeemed by his compassion; what judges us is what redeems us, the love of God. What is it that will break our hearts on judgement day? Is it not the vision, suddenly unrolled, of how he has loved the friends we have neglected, of how he has loved us, and we have not loved him in return; how, when we came before his altar, he gave us himself, and we gave him half-penitences, or resolutions too weak to commit our wills? But while love thus judges us by being what it is, the same love redeems us by effecting what it does. Love shares flesh and blood with us in this present world, that the eyes which look us through at last may find in us a better substance than our vanity.

Advent is a coming, not our coming to God, but his to us. We cannot come to God, he is beyond our reach; but he can come to us, for we are not beneath his mercy. Even in another life, as St. John sees it in his vision, we do not rise to God, but he descends to us, and dwells humanly among human creatures, in the glorious man, Jesus Christ. And that will be his last coming; so we shall be his people, and he everlastingly our God, our God-with-us, our Emmanuel. He *will* so come, but he is come already, he comes always: in our fellow-Christian (even in a child, says Christ), in his Word, invisibly in our souls, more visibly in this sacrament. Opening ourselves to him, we call him in: Blessed is he who comes in the name of the Lord; O come, Emmanuel.

Our judge meets us at every step of our way.

NOVEMBER 28

A reading from a sermon on the Gospel for the Second Sunday in Advent by Hugh Latimer on the text: "There will be signs in the sun, the moon, and the stars, and on the earth . . . " St. Luke 21:25

There are some who think that there shall be great eclipses, against the course of nature; and you know that there have been strange things seen in the elements many times. Sometimes there has been seen a ring about the sun; sometimes there have been seen three suns at once; and such like things have been seen in times past: which no doubt signifies that this fearful day is not far off in which Christ will come with his heavenly host, to judge and reward every one of us according to our desserts.

"People will faint from fear and foreboding" (Luke 21:26); people will be wonderfully fearful; they will pine away for fear: and no doubt they will be good people who will be thus troubled, with such a fear of this day: for you know the worldlings care not for that day; yes, they will scant believe that there will be such a day, that there will be another world, or at the least they would not wish that there will be another world. And no doubt there have been here in England many already, who have been so vexed and turmoiled with such fear.

Therefore let us begin to strive and fight now with sin: let us not set all our hearts and minds upon this world; for no doubt this day, whenever it will come, will be wonderfully fearful to all mankind, and especially to the wicked. There will be great alterations at that day; there will be hurly burly, such as you see when someone dies. So will it be at this fearful, horrible day: there will be such alterations of the earth, and the elements; they will lose their former nature, and be endued with another nature.

"Then they will see 'the Son of Man coming in a cloud' with power and great glory (Luke 21:27). Certain it is, that he shall come to judge, but we cannot tell the time when he will come: therefore, seeing that he will come, let us make ready, lest he find us unprepared. And take this for a rule, that as he finds us, so he will judge us. St. Paul says to the Thessalonians, when he speaks of the resurrection of the good, that on the same day the trumpet will blow, and all will rise who died since the world began; "then we who are alive, who are left, will be caught up in the clouds together with them to meet the Lord in the air" (I Thes. 4:17). All those, I say, who are content to strive and fight with sin, who will not be ruled by sin, these will in this way be taken up in the air and meet with Christ, and so will come down with him again. But as for the other sort, who are wicked, and have a delight in wickedness, and will not leave it, but rather go forward in all mischief, they will be left upon the earth with the devils, until they are judged. And after they have received their sentence, they will go to hell with the devil and all his angels, and there be punished for their sins in hellish fire, world without end. I pray God, that we may be of the number of those, who will hear this joyful and most comfortable voice of Christ our Savior when he will say, "Come, you that are blessed by my Father, inherit the kingdom prepared for you from the foundation of the world" (Matt. 25:34).

There are a great number among the Christian people, who, in the Lord's prayer, when they pray, "Thy kingdom come," pray that this day may come; but yet, nonetheless, they are drowned in the world: they say the words with their lips, but they cannot tell the meaning of it; they speak it only with their tongue: which saying is to no purpose. But that man or woman who says these words, "Thy kingdom come," with a faithful heart, no doubt they desire indeed that God will come to judgment, and to amend all things in this world, and to pull down Satan, that old serpent, under our feet. But there are a great number of us who are not ready. Some have lived in this world fifty years, some sixty; yet for all that they are not prepared for his coming; they think always that he will not come yet. But I tell you that though his general coming is not yet, yet for all that he will come one day, and take us out of this world. And, no doubt, if he find us ready, and in the state of salvation, no doubt we shall be saved for ever, world without end. Therefore it is right for every one of us to take heed. Let us not tarry too long with our amendment, lest we come too short.

Fight now with sin.

A reading from a sermon on the Gospel for the Second Sunday in Advent by Hugh Latimer on the text: "There will be signs in the sun, the moon, and the stars, and on the earth . . . " St. Luke 21:25

How is it that the whole world is so deceitful and false? Because every one of us would like to fare well; everyone loves to have good meat and drink, and to go gaily. And when we have not the means to get such things, then we fall to picking and stealing, and to falsehood, and so deceive our neighbors. But our Savior gives us warning that we must eat and drink measurably and soberly, every one of us according to our estate and measure. Further, we should labor and do our business diligently, every one of us in that estate in which God has set us; and let us trust in God, who no doubt will send us increase of our labor.

Therefore Christ adds, "Keep awake and pray" (Mark 14:38). But those sluggards, who spend their time vainly in eating and drinking and sleeping, they please not God; for God commands us to watch, to be mindful, to take heed to ourselves, lest the devil, or the world, or our own flesh, get the victory over us. We are allowed to take our natural sleep; for it is as necessary for us as meat and drink, and we please God as well in that as when we take our food. But we must take heed that we do it as we are appointed to do; for just as God has not ordained meat and drink so that we should play the glutton with it, so likewise the sleep is not ordained, that we should give ourselves to sluggishness or over-much sleeping; for no doubt, when we do so, we will displease God most highly. Christ says not in vain, "Keep awake and pray." He would have us to be watchers, to have at all times in remembrance his coming, and to give ourselves to prayer, so that we may be able to stand before him at this great and fearful day. We should not trust in ourselves, but call upon God, saying, "Lord God Almighty, you have promised to come and judge, the living and dead! We pray you to give us your grace, and the Holy Spirit that we may so live according to your holy commandments, that when you come, you have no cause to show your fearful anger, but rather your loving kindness and mercy on us!"

So likewise, when we go to bed, we should pray that we sleep not in the sleep of sin and wickedness; but rather that we may leave them, and follow God's will and pleasure, and not be led with the desires of this wicked world. Such an earnest mind we should have toward God and so watchful we should be. For I tell you, it is not a trifling matter; it is not a money matter: for our eternal salvation and our damnation hangs upon it. Our nature is to do all things that are possible for us to get silver and gold: how much more then should we endeavor to make ourselves ready toward this day, when it shall not be a money matter but a soul matter. For at that day it will appear most manifestly who they are who will enjoy everlasting life, and who will be thrust into hell. Now as long as we are in this world, we have all one baptism; we all go to the Lord's supper; we all bear the name of Christians: but then it will appear who are the true Christians; and, again, who are the hypocrites or dissemblers.

Well, I pray God will grant us such hearts, that we may look diligently about us, and make ready against his fearful and joyful coming; fearful to those who delight in sin and wickedness, and will not leave them; and joyful to those who repent, forsake their sins, and believe in him: who, no doubt, will come in great honor and glory, and will make all his faithful like him, and will say to those who are chosen to everlasting life, "Come, you that are blessed by my Father, inherit the kingdom prepared for you from the foundation of the world" (Matt. 25:34). Again, to the wicked, who will not live according to his will and pleasure, but follow their own appetites, he will say, "You that are accursed, depart from me into the eternal fire"(Matt. 25:41).

O, what a horrible thing will this be, to depart from him who is the fountain of all goodness and mercy without whom is no consolation, comfort, nor rest, but eternal sorrow and everlasting death. For God's sake, I require you let us consider this, that we may be among those who shall hear, "Come to me"; that we may be among those who shall enjoy eternal life!

Make ready.

Hope

Watchman, tell us of the night,
what its signs of promise are.
Traveler, o'er yon mountain's height,
see that glory-beaming star.
Watchman, does its beauteous ray
aught of joy or hope foretell?
Traveler, yes; it brings the day,
promised day of Israel.

John Bowring

NOVEMBER 30

A reading from a sermon by R. W. Church on the text: "And now faith, hope, and love abide, these three." I Corinthians 13:13

"Faith, hope, love"; these, in St. Paul's analysis, are the characteristic elements of the Christian mind. St. Paul, as we know, in enumerating them, makes one of them the greatest, in order and in nature—"the greatest of these is love." But it is a first and foremost place among equals. All stand together, as nothing else does, in the front rank of the perfections which make Christian goodness. All are equally indispensable in those who would please God and follow Christ.

But why should hope be ranked so high, placed on a level with faith and love? We can understand why faith should be so singled out; it is the foundation of the whole structure of religion; it is the bond between the creature and the invisible Maker and God; it is the special title of our acceptance; it is the ground of our self-devotion and obedience, of our highest and noblest ventures. Still more can we understand it of love, for love brings us near in the essential qualities of character to the one we believe in and worship. Love is the faint and distant likeness of the one who "so loved the world that he gave his only Son" to save it; love must last and live and increase under whatever conditions the regenerate nature exists, the same in substance, however differing in degree in the humblest penitent on earth and in the adoring saint or seraph in the eternal world. But hope is thought of, at first sight, as a self-regarding quality; something which throws forward its desires into the future, and dwells on what it imagines of happiness for itself. And hope, of all things, is delusive and treacherous; it tempts to security and self-deceit; it tempts us to dreams that cannot be realized, which divert us from the necessary and wholesome realities that *do* concern us: it is the mother of half the mistakes, half the fruitless wanderings, half the unhappiness of the world. How is such a quality placed on a level with faith and love? What need have we of encouragement to do what we are only too ready to do of ourselves?

But it is not really strange that St. Paul should raise hope to a Christian temper of the first order. St. Paul was a student of Scripture and of the history of his people and what is on the surface of the Bible is the way in which from first to last it is one unbroken persistent call to hope—to look from the past and present to the future. Its story of uninterrupted tendency is strangely checkered in fact; bright and dark succeed one another with the most unexpected turns—lofty faith and the meanest disloyalty, great achievements and unexpected failure, lessons of the purest goodness and most heartfelt devotion, with the falls and sins of saints, blessing and chastisement, the patience of God, and the incorrigible provocations of God's people. In spite of all that is wonderful and glorious in it, it sounds like the most disastrous and unpromising of stories; and yet that is not its result. For amid the worst and most miserable conditions there is one element which is never allowed to disappear—the strength of a tenacious and unconquerable hope. Hope, never destroyed, however overthrown, never obscured even amid the storm and dust of ruin, is the prominent characteristic of the Old Testament. All leads back to hope—hope of the loftiest and most assured kind, even after the most fatal defeats, of changes which seem beyond remedy. The last word is always hope. If ever it dies, it revives again larger, more confident than before. It is implied in the very language and appeals of despair. Hope spreads its colors over the Sacred Book, whose outlook and interest is always the future, which looks back to the past only as the ground and pledge of the great things to come. So has St. Paul described the purpose and effect of Scripture, for his words are as true of the New Testament as of the Old. He may be said to have characterized Scripture as, above everything, the Book of Hope. "For whatever was written in former days was written for our instruction, so that by steadfastness and by the encouragement of the scriptures we might have hope."

Hope, I say—the temper and virtue answering to and embracing great and worthy things hoped for—elevates and strengthens and inspires. This is why it is one of the great elements of the religious temper; this is why it ranks with faith and love. It is one of the great and necessary springs of full religious action.

All leads back to hope.

DECEMBER 1

A reading from a sermon by R. W. Church on the text: "And now faith, hope, and love abide, these three." I Corinthians 13:13

The most literal fact that God has set before us, the most wonderful future, is within the certain reach of every single one of us: as certainly within our reach, as anything that we know of, which we could obtain tomorrow. This is the plain, clear, certain promise, without which Christianity is a dream and delusion. The life and destiny of each individual runs up to this; this is what we were made for; for this we have been taught, and have received God's grace, and have been tried, and have played our part in the years of time. It is the barest of commonplaces; and yet, I think, to any who have tried to open their minds to its reality and certainty, it must have come with a strange and overpowering force—new on every fresh occasion, like nothing else in the world. For it is one thing to look forward to some great general event, the triumph of the saints of God, the final glory of the great company of the redeemed; one thing to look at all this from the outside, as a spectator by the power of imagination and thought, and quite another when it comes on your mind that you yourself in the far-off ages, you yourself, the very person now on earth, are intended to have your place, your certain and definite place, in all that triumph, in all that blessedness, in all that glory. Yet surely this is the prospect; this, and nothing less. You may put Christianity aside; you may say that such hopes cannot be for human beings; but, if you are a Christian, this in its utmost fulness and reality is what you are to hope for.

This, as no one denies, is what Scripture invites us to believe and to hope. These are no idle exaggerations of rhetoric or fancy, they are the bare words of truth and soberness. It is what we are living for, unless we are living in vain. Have such things been told us for nothing? Are they things to be without a meaning to us? Is it not *simply a duty* to hope; a sin against God's high goodness, a crime against the order of God's teaching, not to hope? Is it not a duty, in solemn and quiet self-recollection, to put before our thoughts that unbroken and continuous line, which joins this very present moment with that hour which certainly is to arrive, when we *must* be changed, when we *may* be changed into the spotless blessedness of the saints of God? You—you yourself—with your trouble, your temptations, your sin, small or great, your conscious weakness, your insensibility and ignorance; yet you yourself are one of those of whom all this wondrous future must come true. There is no blessedness of the human soul, no rest from weariness, no refreshment after toil, no opening of the eyes to beauty never seen by mortal eye, no delight in goodness, no rejoicing in perfect love, no ineffable sense of the sweetness and tenderness of God's mercy— none of these that may not be hoped for; hoped for with all the warrant of the Almighty's promise. And is that great hope to be practically all a blank to us?

It is not to be told how much we lose of strength, of gladness and enlargement of heart, of power to God's service cheerfully and happily, by not realizing and dwelling on the great hopes "set before us." We let ourselves be blinded, fretted, disheartened by the present, because we will not look up and see what is as certain as the present, in the not very distant future.

We, at least, if we are not Christians in vain, can pass on to the great hope which from end to end fills the Bible—the hope which ennobles and gladdens our mortal life; such a hope as carried St. Paul in strength and joy through the long "daily dying" of his apostleship, and burst forth in such impassioned yet most reasonable conviction—"I consider," he says, "that the sufferings of this present time are not worth comparing with the glory about to be revealed to us. . . . For I am convinced that neither death, nor life, nor angels, nor rulers, nor things present, nor things to come, nor powers, nor height, nor depth, nor anything else in all creation, will be able to separate us from the love of God in Christ Jesus our Lord."

This wondrous future must come true.

DECEMBER 2

A reading on Christian hope from a sermon by Frederick Denison Maurice.

I am concerned with the struggle to *hope*. Spirits of cowardice, of self-indulgence will be about us every day, whispering to us the manifold arguments which there are against hope. "Why should you work? What good is to come of it all? Why should you believe? What have you to believe in? Why should you look to be happy? Does it not seem as if all these multitudes were born to be miserable?"

The last is the point at which we should begin our answer to these suggestions. You ask me what title I can make out to happiness? None. You ask me how I can prove myself better than the suffering multitude. I can offer no such proofs. You ask me then what I have to believe in. I answer, "In the one who created all these myriads and me, in the one who has redeemed these myriads and me, in the one who works even in me by the Spirit, to care for these as well as for myself." I believe in the one who brings the light out of darkness every morning, who causes the sun to shine on the just and on the unjust, on the good and on the evil. You ask me what is the good of work? I answer, "If this is my belief, I am bound also to believe that every work from the beginning of the universe until now has been in some way or other for the manifestation of the glory of the One who created it." I am bound to believe that no work of the hands, no work of the brain, has been useless. All students of nature, of history, of language, of the world without or of the world within, so far as they are faithful, so far as they suffer no prejudices of others, no prejudices of their own, to interfere with their search for truth in their own direction, must be a minister of God, one who is contributing in some way to the manifestation of God's glory. Every individual who is toiling honestly in the field or at the loom must be contributing to the manifestation of God's glory. If any are unfaithful or dishonest, God's purpose will be accomplished, but it is our privilege, if we will, to enter into that purpose, to be fellow-workers with God. And those who claim that privilege must cherish hope, must treat as devils and powers of darkness all that would tempt them to despair. Oh what strength lies in the news that we have a right to strip off the old self, corrupt and deluded by its lusts, and to clothe ourselves with the new self, created according to the likeness of God in true righteousness and holiness.

That new self is the real self, the person after God's own heart; the other is the false self, whom we make by denying our proper state, by giving up the life in Christ for the death which is in ourselves. And every act of repentance or turning to God is a resurrection out of that death, is an entrance into that life. The struggle to choose life and not death may be a hard and continuous one; but it is a struggle to hold fast a truth, the struggle not to believe and act a lie.

Hope in our circumstances is not a pleasant luxury, but an intense necessity. We are sent to proclaim an atonement of heaven with earth, of God with humanity. We are to testify of a blood which cleanses from all sin, of a divine Spirit who guides to all good. We must reduce these messages to our own measures. We must explain them away if we may not hope for the complete triumph of good over evil, of life over death. We have no heart or energy in ourselves to anticipate such a triumph. All that we see mocks us when we dream of it. Our refuge must be in the hope of that which we see not—in the God of hope. If we believe that God's love was manifested in Christ, that all the hatred of our race contended against it and did not prevail, we dare not lose hold of this hope, of this God. The language of St. Paul and of St. John may stretch beyond all that we can ask or think, but we have a right to use it. We may say "we know the one in whom we have put our trust and are sure that he is able to guard until that day what we entrust to him." We may be confident that "every enemy of Christ shall be put under His feet." We dare not reject the divine promise that "every creature in heaven and on earth and under the earth and in the sea, and all that is in them" shall be heard saying, "Amen! Blessing and glory and wisdom and thanksgiving and honor and power and might be to our God forever and ever! Amen."

Cherish hope.

Death

Death be not proud, though some have called thee
Mighty and dreadful, for thou art not so;
For those whom thou think'st thou dost overthrow
Die not poor death, nor yet can'st thou kill me;
From rest and sleep, which but thy pictures be,
Much pleasure, then from thee much more must flow;
And soonest our best men to thee do go,
Rest of their bones and soul's delivery;
Thou art slave to fate, chance, kings, and desperate men
And dost with poison, war, and sickness dwell;
And poison and charms can make us sleep as well,
And better than they stroke; why swell'st thou then?
One short sleep past, we wake eternally
And death shall be no more. Death, thou shalt die!

John Donne

DECEMBER 3
A reading from Holy Dying *by Jeremy Taylor.*

A man is a bubble, said the Greek proverb; and Lucian adds that all the world is a storm, and men rise up in their several generations, like bubbles descending from God and the dew of heaven, from a tear and drop of man, from nature and Providence: and some of these instantly sink into the deluge of their first parent, and are hidden in a sheet of water, having had no other business in the world but to be born so that they might be able to die: others float up and down two or three turns, and suddenly disappear, and give their place to others: and those who live longest upon the face of the waters, are in perpetual motion, restless and uneasy; and being crushed with the great drop of a cloud sink into flatness and a froth; the change not being great, it being hardly possible it could be more of a nothing than it was before. So is every human being: we are born in vanity and sin; we come into the world like morning mushrooms, soon thrusting up their heads into the air, and conversing with their kindred of the same production, and just as soon turning into dust and forgetfulness: some of them without any other interest in the affairs of the world except that they made their parents a little glad, and very sorrowful: others ride longer in the storm; perhaps until seven years of vanity has expired, and then perhaps the sun shines hot upon their heads, and they fall into the shades below, into the cover of death and the darkness of the grave to hide them. But if the bubble stands the shock of a bigger drop, and outlives the chances of a child, of a careless nurse, of drowning in a pail of water, of being overlaid by a sleepy servant, or such little accidents, then the young man or woman dances like a bubble, empty and gay, and shines like a dove's neck, or the image of a rainbow, which has no substance, and whose very imagery and colors are fantastic. So they dance out the gaiety of their youth, and are all the time in a storm, and endure only because they are not knocked on the head by a drop of bigger rain, or crushed by the pressure of a load of undigested meat, or quenched by the disorder of an ill-placed humor. To preserve human beings alive in the midst of so many chances and hostilities is as great a miracle as to create one; to preserve them from rushing into nothing, and at first to draw them up from nothing, are equally the result of an almighty power. Therefore the wisdom of the world has debated who may best express the human condition with words signifying vanity and a short abode. Homer calls a human "a leaf," the smallest, the weakest piece of a short-lived, unsteady plant; Pindar speaks of "the dream of a shadow;" another, "the dream of the shadow of smoke;" but St. James spoke by a more excellent spirit, saying, "our life is but a vapour," that is, drawn from the earth by a celestial influence; made of smoke, or the lighter parts of water, tossed with every wind, moved by the motion of a superior body, without virtue in itself, lifted up on high or left below, according as it pleases the sun its foster-father. But it is lighter yet; it is but an "appearing"; a fantastic vapor, an apparition, nothing real: it is not so much as a mist, not the matter of a shower, nor substantial enough to make a cloud; but it is like Cassiopeia's chair, or Pelops' shoulder, or the circles of heaven, phenomena than which you cannot have a word that can signify a truer nothing. And yet the expression is made one degree more diminutive: a "vapor," and "fantastic," or a "mere appearance," and this but for a little while; the very dream, the phantasm disappears in a small time, "like the shadow that departs"; or "like a tale that is told"; or "as a dream, when one awakes." Human beings are so vain, so unfixed, such perishing creatures, that we cannot long last in the scene of fancy: we go off, and are forgotten, like the dream of a distracted person. The sum of all is this: that you are a human being, than whom there is no greater example in the world of heights and depths, of lights and shadows, of misery and folly, of laughter and tears, of groans and death.

We are born in vanity.

DECEMBER 4

A reading from Holy Dying *by Jeremy Taylor.*

All the succession of time, all the changes in nature, all the varieties of light and darkness, the thousand thousands of accidents in the world, and every contingency to every one, preaches our funeral sermon, and calls us to look and see how the old sexton Time throws up the earth, and digs a grave where we must lay our sins or our sorrows, and sow our bodies, till they rise again in a fair or in an intolerable eternity. Every revolution which the sun makes about the world, divides between life and death; and death possesses both those portions by the next morrow; and we are dead to all those months which we have already lived, and we shall never live them over again: and still God makes little periods of our age. First we change our world, when we come from the womb to feel the warmth of the sun. Then we sleep and enter into the image of death, in which state we are unconcerned in all the changes of the world. And if our mothers or our nurses die, or a wild boar destroy our vineyards, or our king is sick, we regard it not, but during that state are as disinterested as if our eyes were closed with the clay that weeps in the bowels of the earth. At the end of seven years our teeth fall and die before us, representing a formal prologue to the tragedy; and still every seven years it is odds but we shall finish the last scene. And when nature, or chance, or vice, takes our body in pieces, weakening some parts and loosening others, we taste the grave and the solemnities of our own funerals, first in those parts that ministered to vice, and next in those that served for ornament, and in a short time even those that served for necessity become use-less, and entangled like the wheels of a broken clock. Baldness is but a dressing to our funerals, the proper ornament of mourning, and of a person entered very far into the regions and possession of death: and we have many more of the same signification; gray hairs, rotten teeth, dim eyes, trembling joints, short breath, stiff limbs, wrinkled skin, short memory, decayed appetite. Every day's neces-sity calls for a reparation of that portion which death fed on all night, when we lay in death's lap, and slept in death's outer cham-bers. Our spirits prey on the daily portion of bread and flesh, and every meal is a rescue from one death, and lays up for another; and while we think a thought, we die; and the clock strikes, and reckons on our portion of eternity. We form our words with the breath of our nostrils, we have the less to live upon for every word we speak.

Thus nature calls us to meditate on death by those things which are the instruments of acting it: and all the variety of God's providence makes us see death everywhere, in all variety of circumstances, and dressed up for all the fancies and the expectation of every single person. Nature hath given us one harvest every year, but death has two: the spring and the autumn send throngs of men and women to charnel-houses; and all the summer long we are recovering from the evils of the spring, till the dog days come, and the Sirian star makes the summer deadly. The fruits of autumn are laid up for all the year's provision, and those who gather them eat and over-eat and die and need them not and are laid up for eternity. And those who escape till winter only stay for another opportunity which the distempers of that quarter minister to them with great variety. Thus death reigns in all the portions of our time; the autumn with its fruits provides disorders for us, and the winter's cold turns them into sharp diseases, and the spring brings flowers to strew on our hearse, and the summer gives green turf and brambles to bind upon our graves. Calentures and surfeit, cold and agues, are the four quarters of the year, and all minister to death; and you can go nowhere without treading upon a dead man's bones.

Meditate on death.

DECEMBER 5

A reading from the sermon "Death's Duel" by John Donne on the text: "To God, the Lord, belongs escape from death." Psalm 68:20

This whole world is but a universal churchyard, but our common grave, and the life and motion that the greatest persons have in it is but as the shaking of buried bodies in their graves by an earthquake. That which we call life is but a week of death, seven days, seven periods of our life spent in dying, a dying seven times over; and there is an end. Our birth dies in infancy, and our infancy dies in youth, and youth and the rest die in age, and age also dies and determines all. Nor do all these, youth out of infancy, or age out of youth, arise as a phoenix out of the ashes of another phoenix formerly dead, but as a wasp or a serpent out of a carrion, or as a snake out of dung. Our youth is worse than our infancy, and our age worse than our youth. Our youth is hungry and thirsty after those sins which our infancy did not know; and our age is sorry and angry, that it cannot pursue those sins which our youth did. And besides, all the way, so many deaths, that is, so many deadly calamities, accompany every condition and every period of this life, that death itself would be an ease to those who suffer them. Yet God has the keys of death, and can let me out at that door, that is, deliver me from the manifold deaths of this world, the every day's death, and every hour's death, by that one death, the final dissolution of body and soul, the end of all.

But is that the end of all? Is that dissolution of soul and body the last death that the body shall suffer? (for we do not speak now of spiritual death). It is not. Though it may be an issue from the manifold deaths of this world, yet it is an entrance into the death of corruption and putrefaction and vermiculation and incineration and dispersion in and from the grave in which every dead man dies over again. Even those bodies that were "the temples of the Holy Ghost" come to this dilapidation, to ruin, to rubbish, to dust. Truly, we must consider this posthumous death, this death after burial, that after God (with whom are the issues of death) has delivered me from the death of the womb, by bringing me into the world, and from the manifold deaths of the world, by laying me in the grave, I must die again in an incineration of this flesh, and in a dispersion of that dust; that that monarch, who spread over many nations alive, must in his dust lie in a corner of that sheet of lead, and there but so long as that lead will last; and that private and retired man, that thought himself his own for ever, and never came forth, must in his dust of the grave be published, and (such are the revolutions of the graves) be mingled in his dust with the dust of every highway and of every dunghill, and swallowed in every puddle and pond: this is the most inglorious and contemptible vilification, the most deadly and peremptory nullification of man, that we can consider.

If we say, can this dust live? perchance it cannot; it may be the mere dust of the earth, which never did live, nor never shall. It may be the dust of that man's worms which did live, but shall no more. It may be the dust of another man, that concerns not him of whom it is asked. This death of incineration and dispersion is, to natural reason, the most irrecoverable death of all; and yet "to God, the Lord, belongs escape from death"; and by re-compacting this dust into the same body, and reanimating the same body with the same soul, he shall in a blessed and glorious resurrection give me such an issue from this death as shall never pass into any other death, but establish me into a life that shall last as long as the Lord of Life himself. Though from the womb to the grave, and in the grave itself, we pass from death to death, yet, as Daniel says, "The Lord our God is able to deliver us, and will deliver us."

God has the keys of death.

DECEMBER 6

A reading from the sermon "Death's Duel" by John Donne on the text: "To God, the Lord, belongs escape from death." Psalm 68:20

It belongs to God, and not to us, to pass a judgement on us at our death, nor should we conclude a dereliction on God's part by the manner of it. Those indications which the physicians receive, and those predictions which they give for death or recovery in the patient, they receive and they give out of the grounds and the rules of the art. But we have no such rule or art to give a prediction of spiritual death and damnation upon any such indication as we see in any dying person; we see often enough to be sorry, but not to despair; we may be deceived both ways: we are likely to comfort ourselves in the death of friends, if it is testified that they went away like lambs, that is, without any reluctance. But, God knows, that may be accompanied with a dangerous insensibility of their present state. Our blessed Savior suffered a "sadness even in his soul to death," and an agony even to a bloody sweat in his body, and expostulations with God, and exclamations upon the cross. Hilary was a devout man and said upon his death-bed, or death-turf (for he was a hermit), "Have you served a good master three-score and ten years, and now are you reluctant to go into his presence?" Yet Hilary was reluctant. Barlaam was a devout man (and a hermit too) and said on the day he died, "Consider this to be the first day's service that ever you did for your Master, to glorify him in a Christian and a constant death; and if your first day be your last day too, how soon do you come to receive your wages!" Yet Barlaam could have been content to have stayed longer. Make no ill conclusions upon anyone's reluctance to die, for the mercies of God work in minutes, and many times insensibly to bystanders, or any other than the party departing. And as to violent deaths inflicted upon malefactors, Christ himself has forbidden us by his own death to make any ill conclusion; for his own death had those impressions in it; he was reputed, he was executed as a malefactor, and no doubt many of those who concurred in his death did believe him to be so.

"The tree lies where it falls" (Eccles. 2:3). 'Tis true, but yet it is not the last stroke that felled the tree, nor the last word nor gasp that qualifies the soul. We pray still for a peaceable life against violent death, and for a time of repentance against sudden death, and for sober and modest assurance against distempered and diffident death, but never make ill conclusions upon persons overtaken with such deaths; "To God, the Lord, belongs escape from death." Our critical day is not the very day of our death, but the whole course of our life. I thank the one who prays for me when my bell tolls, but I thank the one much more who catechizes me, or preaches to me, or instructs me how to live. There's my security, the mouth of the Lord has said it, "do this and you shall live" (Luke 10: 28). But though I do it, yet I shall die too, die a bodily, a natural death. But God never mentions, never seems to consider that death, the bodily, the natural death. God does not say, "Live well, and you shall die well," that is, an easy, a quiet death; but, "Live well here, and you shall live well for ever." As the first part of a sentence fits well with the last, and never respects, never listens to, the parenthesis that comes between, so does a good life here flow into an eternal life, without any consideration of what manner of death we die.

But whether the gate of my prison be opened with an oiled key (by a gentle and preparing sickness), or the gate be hewn down by a violent death, or the gate be burnt down by a raging and frantic fever, a gate into heaven I shall have, for from the Lord is the cause of my life, and "to God, the Lord, belongs escape from death." God cares that the soul be safe, whatever agonies the body suffers in the hour of death.

God cares that the soul be safe.

DECEMBER 7

A reading from "The Last Great Adventure," a sermon by Charles Henry Brent on the text: "Beloved, we are God's children now; what we will be has not yet been revealed. What we do know is this: when he is revealed, we will be like him, for we will see him as he is." I St. John 3:2

I have wondered at times whether the Church has not over-mysticized the conception of life beyond the grave, and, in so doing, made death not an incident but a break in life. The book of the Apocalypse is the basis of most pictures of the other world. Its oriental color and richness, its deep symbolism, its figurative mode of expression are foreign to Western thought and method. It has not been translated enough, and we have failed to get the purport of its mystical measures. Our untrained imaginations have fallen a prey to literalism. I am not objecting to the glow of mystery which is part of the charm and part of the reality of any attempt to depict that which is interior to and beyond our life and experience. Nor is it desirable to express the other world in terms of this. What is necessary, however, is to leave no room to suppose that after death we are any different than we were before in our inmost self, to accentuate the continuity of life, and to keep all artificiality out of the picture of the great beyond.

The first and best illustration of the effect upon personality of death is found in Jesus Christ. After his reappearance from the grave, he is unaltered in character, tone of thought, and fundamental relationships. What strikes one forcibly is the absence of anything like a break in the continuity of his personality.

If we think of death as an introduction into conditions wholly foreign and unsuited to human nature, death must be something to be feared. It is unwanted in that it is untried. But it is thoroughly human in that it is part of universal human experience. It is suited to us. It is the next thing we need when we have finished here. Our Lord promises by his own representative career what will happen to us. Of course the resurrection and all it means still lie beyond, but the interim period is as well fitted to human life as the post-resurrection period.

Dante does a great service in the *Divine Comedy* by his method. He carries earth down to the Inferno and up to the Purgatorio and the Paradiso. The language used and the country depicted are such as are familiar. The mystical is not absent, but it is not overwhelming.

Then as to our nearer relationship with God. We use the phrase *beatific vision* to indicate that complete realization of God's presence and our nearness to God which is the greatest gift of heaven. After death the earliest impact of God, so to speak, will be God's self-giving, God's tender love. Julian of Norwich is always eloquent on this last point. In her sixth revelation, which is one of the choicest, she pictures God's appreciation of what God's children do. "The good Lord said: *I thank thee for thy travail, and especially for thy youth.*" Her vision is of our Lord as lord in his own house entertaining his dear worthy servants and friends at a stately feast. His humility is the first thing she noticed—the Lord took no place in his house, but he reigned there royally, filling it full of joy and mirth, "Himself endlessly to gladden and to solace his dear worthy friends, full homely and full courteously, with marvelous melody of endless love, in his own fair blessed countenance." Then she describes the three degrees of bliss that every "soul shall have in heaven that willingly served God in any degree on earth." The first is the worshipful thanks of our Lord God—you see he is not exacting but giving—the second is that the thanks are made publicly in the presence of all heaven. "A king, if he thank his servants, it is a great worship to them, and if he makes it known to all the realm, then is the worship greatly increased." And the third is, that "as new and as gladdening as it is received in that time, right so shall it last without end."

It is not because I believe there is absence of discipline beyond the grave when we have achieved the last adventure that I have given chief place to the gentle courtesy of God, but because the thought of God's austerity can be borne only upon the background of God's mercy. Such discipline there is. I know I shall need it. Our own sense of justice will welcome it. Whatever it may be we have no reason to fear it, for it will be but a single element in the great bath of God's love which will receive us, and will be exactly that which we need to shape us into the sort of persons we most desire to be.

We have no reason to fear.

A reading from a sermon of Phillips Brooks on the text: "And I saw the dead, great and small, standing before the throne." Revelation 20:12

The life which we are living now is more aware than we know of the life which is to come. Death, which separates the two, is not, as it has been so often pictured, like a great thick wall. It is rather like a soft and yielding curtain, through which we cannot see, but which is always waving and trembling with the impulses that come out of the life which lies upon the other side of it. We are never wholly unaware that the curtain is not the end of everything. Sounds come to us, muffled and dull, but still indubitably real, through its thick folds. Every time that a new soul passes through that veil from mortality to immortality, it seems as if we heard its light footfalls for a moment after the jealous curtain has concealed it from our sight. As each soul passes, it almost seems as if the opening of the curtain to let it through were going to give us a sight of the unseen things beyond; and, though we are forever disappointed, the shadowy expectation always comes back to us again, when we see the curtain stirred by another friend's departure. After our friend has passed, we can almost see the curtain, which he stirred, moving, tremulously for a while, before it settles once more into stillness.

Behind this curtain of death, St. John, in his great vision, passed, and he has written down for us what he saw there. He has not told us many things; and probably we cannot know how great the disappointment must have been if he had tried to translate into our mortal language all the ineffable wonders of eternity. But he has told us much; and most of what we want to know is wrapped up in this simple and sublime declaration, "'I saw the dead, small and great, stand before God.'"

I think that it grows clearer and clearer to us all that what we need are the great truths, the vast and broad assurances within which are included all the special details of life. Let us have them, and we are more and more content to leave the special details unknown. With regard to eternity, for instance, I am sure that we can most easily, nay, most gladly, forego the detailed knowledge of the circumstances and occupations of the other life, if only we can fully know two things—that the dead are, and that they are with God. All beside these two things we can most willingly leave undiscovered. And those two things, if we can believe St. John, are sure.

The dead are with God.

Judgment

Day of wrath! O day of mourning!
See fulfilled the prophets' warning,
Heaven and earth in ashes burning.

O what fear man's bosom rendeth
When from heaven the Judge descendeth
On whose sentence all dependeth!

Wondrous sound the trumpet flingeth;
Through earth's sepulchers it ringeth;
All before the throne it bringeth.

Death is struck, and nature quaking,
All creation is awaking,
To its Judge an answer making.

Lo! The book exactly worded,
Wherein all hath been recorded:
Thence shall judgment be awarded.

When the Judge his seat attaineth
And each hidden deed arraigneth,
Nothing unavenged remaineth.

Latin, 13th century
possibly by Thomas of Celano
translated by William J. Irons, 1849

DECEMBER 9

A reading from a sermon by Mark Frank.

There were in the Apostles' times, and there are still in ours, men who loved to scare the people with prophecies and dreams of the end of the world, as if this "then" already were at hand; such as would define the year and day, as if they had lately dropped out of God's council-chamber; but "we beg you," says St. Paul, "not to be quickly shaken in mind or alarmed, either by spirit or by word or by letter, as though from us, to the effect that the day of the Lord is already here. Let no one deceive you" (II Thess. 2:2–3); "they only deceive you, they vent their own dreams and fond presumptions. They know not when the Master of the house will come, in the evening, or at midnight, or at cockcrow, or at dawn"(Mark 13:35), "for like a trap . . . it will come upon all who live on the face of the whole earth" (Luke 21:35).

It is enough for us to know there shall be a day of judgment, against which we must provide every day to make up our accounts, lest that day come upon us unawares, lest death at last hurry us away to our particular doom, which will leave us where the last judgment will be sure to find us, in the same condition; no power or tears of ours being then able to change or alter it. So that the punctual time of this coming, as Christ did not intend to declare, so it matters not to know.

For "we will all stand before the judgment seat of God."

A "then," a time there will be of his coming, a time when "they will see" him come; and who are "they" but all mankind? "Every eye will see him, even those who pierced him" (Rev. 1:7); who crucified him, and condemned him," says Christ himself, to those who were his torturers and his judges. "From now on you will see the Son of Man seated at the right hand of Power" (Matt. 26:64). Nay, "we will all stand before the judgment seat of God" (Rom. 14:10). None of us all must think to escape. There we must give account what we have done amiss: every action, every idle word, every vain and wanton inward desire, must we yield account of in the end. Your crown and throne, O king, cannot exempt you! Your honours and compliments, O nobles, cannot excuse you! Your riches, O son of wealth, cannot buy your absence! Your deceits, O crafty politician, cannot evade it! Your strength, O soldier, cannot defend you from the angel that will drive you thither. Your learning, O learned of the earth, can find no argument to keep you from it. Nor can you, O you worms of the earth, find holes in it to hide you at this coming.

Come you must all together at this coming, and see you shall the Son of man as he is coming. The wicked eyes, indeed, though Christ comes in glory, shall see nothing of his glory. The Son of man they shall behold, his humanity, but not his Deity. They shall see the wounds their sins have made, the hands and feet they have nailed, the side they have pierced, the head they have pressed with thorns; all these to their grief and sorrow, to see him their Judge, whom they have so abused and wronged, so trampled and scorned, that he yet bears the marks of their malice and cruelty even in his throne of glory.

But the good man's eyes shall see his glory too; they shall behold his glorious face, which the eyes of the sinners and the ungodly are not able to perceive, because of that veil of sin and darkness that covers them. Both, then, shall see him; these only the Son of man, those the Son both of God and man, in his cloud, and in his glory.

Who are they, then, who think to hide themselves, who live as if they never thought to come to judgment? Did men certainly but seriously ponder that, will they nill they, they must one day see Christ, they would use him better in his members than they do; better in his church and ministers; better in his worship and service. Do they not, think you, imagine they shall never see him?—that they can shelter themselves somewhere from his presence—that dare use him thus contemptuously, thus proudly, thus sacrilegiously and profanely? Lay just this close every day to your bosoms as you rise: that you must one day come to appear before him; and all your actions will be more regular, and your thoughts higher concerning Christ, and all that is his, or pertains to him; and you the better able to answer them when you see him.

We must give account.

DECEMBER 10

A reading from a sermon of Phillips Brooks on the text: "And I saw the dead, great and small, standing before the throne." Revelation 20:12

"The dead, small and great," St. John says that he saw standing before God. In that great judgment day, another truth is that the difference of sizes among human lives, of which we make so much, passes away, and all human beings, in simple virtue of their human quality, are called to face the everlasting righteousness. The child and the greybeard, the scholar and the boor, however their lives may have been separated here, they come together there. It is upon the moral ground that the most separated souls must always meet. Upon the child and the philosopher alike rests the common obligation not to lie, but to tell the truth. The scholar and the plowboy both are bound to be pure and to be merciful. Differently as they may have to fulfil their duties, the duties are the same for both. Intellectual sympathies are limited. The more we study, the more we separate ourselves into groups with special interests. But moral sympathies are universal. The more we try to do right, the more we come into communion with all the others who are engaged in the same struggle all through the universe. Therefore it is that before the moral judgment seat of God all souls, the small and great, are met together.

All may be good—all may be bad; therefore, before the One whose nature is the decisive touchstone of goodness and badness in every nature which is laid upon it, all souls of all the generations of mankind may be assembled. Think what a truth that is. We try to find some meeting ground for all humanity, and what we find is always proving itself too narrow or too weak. The one only place where all can meet, and every soul claim its relationship with every other soul, is before the throne of God. The Father's presence alone furnishes the meeting place for all the children, regardless of differences of age or wisdom. The grave and learned of this earth shall come up there before God, and find, standing in God's presence, that all which they have truly learned has not taken them out of the sympathy of the youngest and simplest of their Father's children. On the other hand, the simple child, who has timidly gazed afar off upon the great minds of his race, and who comes to stand with them before God, will not be shut out from them. Even that child has a key which will unlock their doors and allow an entrance into their lives. Because they are all obeying the same God, that child also has some part in the eternal life of Abraham, and Moses, and Paul. Not directly, but through the God before whom both of them stand, the small and great come together. The humility of the highest and the self-respect of the lowest are both perfectly attained. The children, who have not been able to understand or hold communion with each other directly, meet perfectly together in the Father's house, and the dead, small and great, stand in complete sympathy and oneness before God.

All come together before God.

DECEMBER 11

A reading from a sermon of Phillips Brooks on the text: "And I saw the dead, great and small, standing before the throne." Revelation 20:12

And now one question still remains! Is the fulfilment of the vision of St. John for us to wait for until we are dead? Can only the dead stand before God? Think for a moment what we found to be the blessings of that standing before God, and then consider that those privileges, however they may be capable of being given more richly to the human soul in the eternal world, are privileges upon whose enjoyment any soul may enter here. Consider this, and the question at once is answered. Already, now, you and I may live by the standards of the eternal righteousness, and we may claim our fellowship with the least and the greatest of our fellow human beings, and we may so lay hold on God that we shall realize our immortality. The soul that has done all that, is now standing before God. It does not need to push aside the curtain, and to enter into the unknown world which lies behind. While we are living here, walking these common streets, living in closest intercourse with others, we are already in the everlasting presence, and our heaven has begun.

But now these are the very things which Jesus Christ promises to give, and which he has given to multitudes. All who will come to him and serve him are brought thereby to the loftiest standards of righteousness, to the broadest and deepest human fellowship, and to such a true knowledge of God that their own immortality becomes real to them.

Is it not true, then, that Christ does for the soul which follows him, that which the experience of the eternal world shall take up and certify, and complete? Already in him we begin to live the everlasting life. Already its noble independence, its deep discrimination, its generous charity, its large hopefulness, its great abounding and inspiring peace gathers around and fills the soul which lives in obedience to him. Already, as he himself said, "Whoever believes in the Son has eternal life."

And yet, while we need not wait till we are dead for the privilege and power of "standing before God," yet still the knowledge of that loftier and more manifest standing before God, which is to come in the unseen land, of which St. John has told us, may make more possible the true experience of the divine presence which we may have here. Because I am to stand before God in some yet unimagined way, seeing God with some keener sight, hearing God's words with some quicker hearing which shall belong to some new condition of eternity, therefore I will be sure that my true life here consists in such a degree of realization of God's presence, such a standing before God in obedience, and faith, and love, as is possible for one in this lower life.

When the change comes to any of us, my friends, how little it will be, if we have really been, through the power of Jesus Christ, standing before God, in our poor, half-blind way upon the earth. If now, in the bright freshness of your youth, you give yourself to Christ, and through him do indeed know God as your dearest friend, years and years hence, when the curtain is drawn back for you, and you are bidden to join the host of the dead who stand before God eternally, how slight the change will be. Only the change from the struggle to the victory, only the opening of the dusk and twilight into the perfect day. "Well done, good and trustworthy slave; you have been trustworthy in a few things, I will put you in charge of many things; enter into the joy of your master."

We are already in God's presence.

DECEMBER 12

A reading from a sermon by John Keble on a text from St. Matthew:
"His winnowing fork is in his hand, and he will clear his threshing
floor and will gather his wheat into the granary; but the chaff he will
burn with unquenchable fire." St. Matthew 3:12

The immediate effect of Christ's coming will be like winnowing.
Only come to him seriously in faith, and you will hear him call your
names over from his glorious throne and he will store you up with
the best of his wheat in the garner. "But the chaff he will burn with
unquenchable fire." It will not only be driven away, but burned.
The breath of the Lord, which will separate the good corn from the
refuse, will prove like a stream of brimstone, to kindle a fire on
what it drives away. And, once kindled, that fire will never go out.
Scripture calls it everlasting, unquenchable, and says plainly, that
"the smoke of their torment goes up forever and ever" (Rev. 14:11).

O fearful to think of, what some of us may know but too certainly, that we should ourselves have ever been scorched with the
flame of that fire, should willfully have gone near, and so trifled
with it, that, had we died as we then were, it must have been our
portion for ever. And yet this is the case with all of us, who have
willfully cast ourselves into deadly sin, or knowingly continued in
it. And, O yet more fearful and distressing, should any of us even
now be in that same condition, secretly or openly going on in any
of the things of which it is said, "Those who do such things will not
inherit the kingdom of God" (Gal. 5:21). Such persons have already,
in a manner, the fire of hell kindled upon them, and they know it
not. They go about perhaps gaily among us, but what if in the sight
of God and the angels they should even now seem to be wrapped
in those horrible flames? Fire unquenchable; everlasting burnings;
can we hear of it, and not be moved? Shall God draw near, God our
Savior, to tell us of it, and shall we not even begin examining ourselves, whether it has kindled upon us or no? For if we are in any of
those deadly sins, be sure it has kindled upon us though as yet,
blessed be God, it may be quenched by the waters of repentance
and the blood of the cross. The Lord of the harvest stands by with
his fan in his hand, and tells us what he will do with the wheat, and
what with the chaff; and shall we not even consider whether we

ourselves are not chaff rather than wheat? What is chaff ? It is a light, worthless thing, easily blown about by every wind: it has no life, no power, no substance in it. Would that we had not, very many of us, too great cause to fear that our religion, during great part of our lives, has been no more real than this.

And what shall we say to those who, from time to time have formed in their hearts good and holy purposes; good and holy, if they had but been kept; and from time to time, alas! have broken them so that while they seemed to themselves always intending to grow better, they have been always relapsing into the same faults, or worse. Surely these also are chaff; they cannot be good corn; there can be nothing in them to please the watchful husbandman. They are chaff; else they would not so lightly swerve from what they had promised themselves to do; they would not break through a good custom, such as going a long distance to church and communion, merely because it gave them trouble; they would not let troublesome or plausible talkers persuade them out of ways which they know to be right, even if they cannot explain how. Above all, they would be strong against positive temptations to known sin.

These, my friends, are the sort of marks by which the Lord of the harvest will try us, when he sets about purging his floor. By these therefore let us try ourselves now; now, during this very week, during the little time yet remaining of Advent. For why should the Judge come, and after so many warnings find us at last unprepared? Why should Christmas come and go, and leave us as little in earnest, as heartless and unthankful as ever to our loving Savior? Why should new years, one after another, arise on us, and we still continue like chaff, light, useless, unsteady, and fit only to be burned at last?

Shall we not examine ourselves?

Hell

When, go ye, cursed, God proclaims,
And sinners plunge in endless flames,
Think, O my soul, what mighty pain,
    The damned sustain.

Self-rage for breach of gracious laws,
The worm of conscience which still gnaws,
Confusion, terror, trembling, shame,
    And fierce self-blame.

Heaven lost, the choice of torments sure,
Souls tempered tortures to endure,
Gnashing of teeth, outrageous fire,
    And darkness dire.

How long have I 'gainst God rebelled?
How many gracious calls repelled?
More hardships ran to work my bane
    Than heaven would gain.

My pestilence I oft diffused,
Great God's long suffering I abused,
And damned to these eternal woes,
    Have what I chose.

All praise to God who spares me time,
To search and mourn for every crime;
Souls armed with penitential tear,
    Hell never fear.

Thomas Ken

DECEMBER 13

A reading from a sermon by Edward Bouverie Pusey on the text: "And these will go away into eternal punishment, but the righteous into eternal life." St. Matthew 25:46

Place alone does not make heaven or hell. Hell, with the love of God, would be like heaven; without the love of God, it may be, it seems even probable, that heaven would be the worse hell. Hell may be the less misery to the damned. For to be in heaven and yet to be as a devil, to see the mutual bliss of creatures such as we once were, yet from our own hateful passions to be incapable of it, to see their joy in God and the beatific unfolding of God's essence to their transported gaze, and ourselves, being such as we had unmade ourselves, incapable of any love or joy—the contrast of such bliss and such misery, such love and such hate, seems the worse hell.

Do you think it is impossible to see God and to hate God? God forbid, that we should be able to conceive it! Yet we see it in Satan. There is no middle line in the end between loving God and hating God. "Haters of God" is one of the habitual forms of human nature left to itself. When God took flesh and dwelt among us "full of grace and truth," this was the witness the truth bore of us. "Whoever hates me hates my Father also. If I had not done among them the works that no one else did, they would not have sin. But now they have seen and hated both me and my Father" (John 15:23–24). But hatred of God is in itself hell.

We were created for love, the love of our God, and of each other in God. To exist without love, without loving, without being loved, would in itself be unendurable misery. It would be an unnatural existence, which must be restless and miserable because unnatural and missing that for which it was created. Not to love, is to hate: "For we ourselves," says St. Paul of unregenerate nature, "were once foolish, disobedient, led astray, slaves to various passions and pleasures, passing our days in malice and envy, despicable, hating one another" (Titus 3:3).

Apart from the central misery, the endless loss of the end of our being, of the one who is still our God; apart from all those terrific physical miseries, of which our Lord speaks, the inextinguishable fire, the never-dying worm of each—the society of the damned would be misery unutterable. Conceive this alone, to which, St. Paul says human nature of itself went, hatred of God, intrinsic hatefulness, hatred of one another. Gather in one in your mind an assembly of all those men or women, from whom, whether in history or in fiction, your memory most shrinks (no fiction can reach the reality of human sin); gather in mind all which is most loathsome, most revolting, the most treacherous, malicious, coarse, brutal, inventive, fiendish cruelty, unsoftened by any remains of human feeling; such as you could not endure for a single hour; conceive the fierce, fiery eyes of hate, spite, frenzied rage, ever fixed on you, glaring on you, looking you through and through with hate; sleepless in their horrible gaze; felt, if not seen; never turning from you, never to be turned from, except to quail under the like piercing sight of hate; hear those yells of blaspheming concentrated hate, as they echo along the lurid vault of hell; everyone hating everyone, and venting that hate unceasingly with every inconceivable expression of malignity; conceive all this, multiplied, intensified, reflected all around, on every side; and, amid it, the especial hatred of anyone whose sins you shared, whom you thoughtlessly encouraged in sin, or taught some sin before unknown—a deathlessness of hate would be in itself everlasting misery. Yet a fixedness in that state, in which the hardened, malignant sinner dies, involves, without any further retribution of God, this endless misery.

To exist without loving would be unendurable.

A reading from Introductory Papers on Dante *by Dorothy L. Sayers.*

It is the deliberate choosing to remain in illusion and to see God and the universe as hostile to one's ego that is of the very essence of hell. The dreadful moods when we hug our hatred and misery and are too proud to let them go are foretastes in time of what hell eternally is. So long as we are in time and space, we can still, by God's grace and our own wills assenting, repent of hell and come out of it. But if we carry that determination and that choice through the gates of death into the state in which there is, literally, no time, what then? Death, which was the bitter penalty attached to our knowledge of evil, is also our privilege and opportunity. We are not allowed just to slip away easily, body and soul, into eternity, as the early fathers imagined we might have done if we had never lost our innocence. In knowing evil, we had to know death as a crisis—the sharp sundering of mortal and immortal—and in that crisis we see the choice between reality and illusion.

As it passes out of the flesh the soul sees God and sees its own sin. This crisis and confrontation are technically known as the Particular Judgment. If, in the very moment of that crisis, the true self is still alive, however feebly: if, deep down beneath all perversities of self-will, the absolute will is still set towards God's reality, and the soul can find it in itself, even at that last moment, to accept judgment—to fling away the whole miserable illusion and throw itself upon truth, then it is safe. It will have to do in purgatory, with incredible toil and without the assistance of the body, the training which it should have done on earth: but in the end it will get to where it truly wants to be. There is no power in this world or the next that can keep a soul from God if God is what it really desires. But if, seeing God, the soul rejects God in hatred and horror, then there is nothing more that God can do for it. God, who has toiled to win it, and borne for its sake to know death, and suffer the shame of sin, and set foot in hell, will nevertheless, if it insists, give it what it desires. The people who think that if God were truly nice and kind, God would let us have everything we fancy, are really demanding that God should give us freehold of hell. And if that is our deliberate and final choice, if with our whole selves we are determined to have nothing but self, God will, in the end, say, "Take it." God cannot, against our own will, force us into heaven, in the spirit of "I've brought you out to enjoy yourself and you've got to enjoy yourself." Heaven would then be a greater agony than hell— or rather, hell *is* heaven as seen by those who reject it: just as the agonies of the jealous *are* love, seen through the distorting illusion.

We might adapt the definition of Boethius and say: "Hell is the perfect and simultaneous possession of one's own will for ever."

God cannot force us into heaven.

DECEMBER 15

A reading from Devout Exercises of the Heart *by Elizabeth Rowe.*

What is hell, what is damnation, but an exclusion from your presence? 'Tis the loss of that which gives the regions of darkness all their horror. O when will you scatter this melancholy darkness? When will the shadows flee before you? When will the cheerful glory of your grace dawn upon my mind at your approach? I will revive at your light; my vital spirits will confess your presence. Grief and anxiety will vanish before you, and immortal joys surround my soul.

Where you are present, heaven and happiness ensue; hell and damnation fills the breast where you are absent. While God withdraws I am encompassed with darkness and despair; the sun and stars shine with an uncomfortable luster; the faces of my friends grow tiresome; the smile of angels would fail to cheer my languishing spirit. I grow unacquainted with tranquility; peace and joy are empty sounds to me, and words without a meaning.

Tell me not of glory and pleasure—there are no such things without God. When God withdraws, what delight can these trifles afford? All that amuses mankind are but dreams of happiness, shadows, and fantasies. What compensation can they make for an infinite good departed? All nature cannot repair my loss; heaven and earth would offer their treasures in vain. Not all the kingdoms of this world, nor the thrones of archangels, could give me a recompense for an absent God.

O where can my grief find redress? Whence can I draw satisfaction, when the fountain of joy seals up its streams? My sorrows are hopeless till God return. Without God my night will never see a dawn, but extend to everlasting darkness. Contentment and joy will be eternal strangers to my breast. Had I all things within the compass of creation to delight me, God's frowns would blast the whole enjoyment. Unreconciled to God, my soul would be forever at variance with itself.

Even now, while I believe your glory hidden from me with only a passing eclipse, and while I wait for your return as for the dawning day, my soul suffers inexpressible agonies at the delay. The minutes seem to linger and the days are lengthened into ages. But Lord, what keener anguish should I feel if I thought your presence had totally forsaken me, if I imagined your glory should no more arise on my soul! My spirits fail at the thought: I cannot face the dreadful apprehensions of my God forever gone. Is it not hell in its most horrid prospect, eternal darkness and the undying worm, infinite ruin and irreparable damage? Compared to this, what were all the plagues that earth could threaten or hell invent? What are disgrace, and poverty, and pain? What are all that mortals fear, real or imaginary evils?

They are nothing compared to the terrors raised by the thought of losing my God. O Lord, you are my boundless treasure, my infinite delight, my all, my ineffable portion; how can I part with you? I may see without light and breathe, without air, sooner than be blessed without my God. Happiness separate from you is a contradiction, an impossibility (if I dare speak it) to Omnipotence itself. I feel a flame which the most glorious creation could not satisfy, an emptiness which nothing but infinite love could fill. I must find you or weary myself in an eternal pursuit. Nothing shall divert me in the endless search, no obstacle shall frighten me back, no allurement withhold me; nothing shall flatter or relieve my impatience. My bliss, my heaven, my all depends on my success in this. Show me where you are, O my God; conduct me into your presence, and let my love confine me there forever.

Show me where you are, O my God.

Heaven

Nor eye, ear, thought, can take the height
To which my song is taking flight,
   Yet raised an humble wing,
   My guess of heaven I'll sing;
'Tis love's reward, and love is fired
By guessing at the bliss desired.

Guess then at saints' eternal lot,
By due considering what 'tis not,
   No misery, want, or care,
   No death, no darkness there,
No troubles, storms, sighs, groans, or tears,
No injury, pains, sickness, fears.

They dwell in pure ecstatic light,
Of God Triune have blissful sight,
   Of fontal love who gave
   God filial man to save,
Of Jesus' love, who death sustained,
By which the saints their glory gained.

Thomas Ken

DECEMBER 16

A reading from The Religious Vocation *by R. M. Benson.*

The joy that binds together the saints in the blessed community of eternal life is a joy of perfect sympathy since all are pouring forth their whole being to the One who is the center of their conceptions, and the common principle of their life. They turn not aside from God to speak one to another; their whole being is rapt in the thought of God, and they live in the knowledge of the mutual love which binds them all because that love binds each to God, and the very power of love whereby each is bound to God is an undivided power. They live there, not as separate individuals existing according to the law of their own consciousness; but there they have a perfect life as members of one living body, living with one undivided act of life. There they live for ever perfected in one, and their whole being is but the temple of the eternal Word. All their movements are hushed, all their words and thoughts have ceased, everything that is transitory has passed away for ever. Their common consciousness is the changeless and eternal consciousness of God, as the central principle of life; a consciousness eternal, that never can be exhausted, and changeless, for it knows no accident, but in its eternal changelessness ever knowing itself with a freshness of perfect delight; changeless and free from all the novelty of changeful time, changeless in all the perfect freshness of the never-wearying life of God.

Eternity is the manifestation of the marvelous unification of life. None can possess anything in eternity, and have it simply as their own property; each one has it for the well-being of the whole. No individuals can be partakers of that life, and live within the sphere of their own simple thoughts. The life of heaven is a self-communicating life; it is the life of God. And as the Father gives the fullness of life to the Son, and the Father and the Son give the fullness of their life to the Holy Ghost, so each one of us dwelling in the power of the same Spirit must be continually giving forth that life: we cannot live in it upon any other terms.

In the revelation of the Spirit there is that perfect identity of being, so that all are really and truly one. No distance of separation, of climate, or of age; no distance which may have separated us upon earth; no distance of perfection to which we may have attained, is between ourselves and the great apostolic saints. No distance has any reality, for all are perfectly one; one undivided act of love thrilling through all. Each individual is a center of spiritual emanations, while yet that Spirit which emanates from each is an undivided Spirit; for there is the perfect indwelling of the Holy Ghost, dwelling in each according to measure, yet suffering no division while God's power is communicated to each.

Oh, the wondrous light of that city! There is no darkness there; no intervening darkness to separate one saint from another, for all are built up in the being of Christ, and the light of each individual saint shines forth, mingling itself in the fullness of the eternal light with the light which shines from the thousands and thousands that are around. There is distinction without distance, there is multiplicity without bewilderment, and there is mingling without confusion. Yes, there is a marvelous reciprocity of joy there with which all the saints give forth their luster, and rejoice in the manifestation of their own experience of the divine love, while they rejoice equally in the manifestation of the divine love as it has been experienced, realized, and exhibited by all around. And as the pure white light is a combination of many rays of color, so in the purity of the city of God there is a combination of manifold rays of color. As there is the threefold personality of the eternal Trinity, which is the basis of the heavenly light, so there is the marvelous multiplicity of all the saints, in whom this light shines forth reflected; and as it shines forth reflected, it shines forth in perfect unity.

There is no darkness in Christ.

A reading from a sermon by Edward Bouverie Pusey on the text: "But our citizenship is in heaven." Philippians 3:20

"Our citizenship is in heaven." Many are the meanings of this word, and every way the Apostle says we are in heaven. For the word, in the original language, means the city or state to which we belong, or the way of life of the citizens, and in all these ways he places us in heaven. He does not say only, our faith, our hopes, our expectation, the object of our longing, is in heaven; he speaks not of what is to be, but of what is; "our citizenship *is* in heaven." Again, he does not say, "it ought to be," "let it be," "let our deeds and words and thoughts aim thitherward, thither aspire, thither be directed"; he does not even say, "we live on earth a holy and heavenly life, a life after the manner of the blessed angels," nor " thither we aim, thither stretch forward, thither we hope to attain to Christ, who has prepared the way for us, and is himself the Way; nor does he say, "we are *as it were*, citizens of heaven, living under heavenly rule, heavenly laws, all of which breathes of heaven"; nor even, "we are in the kingdom of heaven, a heaven upon earth," as the Apostle saw "the Holy City," the church, "the heavenly Jerusalem," come down from God out of heaven. All this is true of God's chosen ones; all, through God's grace, might be true of us; but here he speaks of no hope of things to come, no aim, no likeness, no blessedness, on earth; but of that which is; "our citizenship is" (not *of*, nor *like*, nor *tending* to) but "*in* heaven."

Let us think of the words awhile in these different ways. "Our citizenship," in a word, our home "is in heaven." Yet so it might be, so, in one sense, it is, though we were away from home. For, as the Apostle says, "While we are present in the body, we are absent from the Lord." Yet it is not altogether an absent home of which the Apostle speaks. He does not say, our home is far away, as that to which we have no access, as our home might be beyond the seas, or the vast stormy ocean of this world. He speaks not of our home as something separate from us, not as something in space in which we might be and are not, but as something belonging to us, and to which we belong, to which of right (not our own surely, but as by Christ Jesus purchased for us), and in fact, we belong. For the temple, of God, the church, is not made with hands, not a material building, as this wherein we worship God, so that if it is here, it cannot be there, if in heaven, not on earth. One church we know it is, of all who are, or have been, or shall be, in Christ Jesus, all, wherever they are, in heaven or in earth, all, human beings and angels, knit in one in him. And in this we are fellow-citizens; "strangers and pilgrims" on earth, in the body, because our affections are not here; "not strangers and foreigners, but fellow-citizens of the saints, and of the household of God," living with and under God, guarded, fed, maintained by him; yes, having a holy boldness and familiar reverent intercourse with God, as members of God's family, God's great household. And this perhaps will contain in one all the meaning of this word, that we are inhabitants, citizens, of heaven, not of earth. To earth we belong as to these poor bodies, which shall return to the earth, because not as yet has Christ come to "transform the body of our humiliation that it may be conformed to the body of his glory, by the power that also enables him to make all things subject to himself" (Phil. 3:21), "and raised us up with him and seated us with him in the heavenly places" (Eph. 2:6), but as yet not in body but in soul. But in soul and spirit, he would say, we are there already. There life centers, there we live; to it we belong. *There* are your goods, and treasures; your rights, your possessions, your kindred, your friends, your dwelling place.

There we live.

DECEMBER 18

A reading from a sermon by Richard Baxter on texts from the First Epistle to the Corinthians: "Flesh and blood cannot inherit the kingdom of God." "You do not sow the body that is to be, but . . . God gives it a body as he has chosen, and to each kind of seed its own body." I Corinthians 15:50; 15:37, 38

As the ore is cast into the fire a stone, but comes forth so pure a metal that it deserves another name, and so the difference between the stone and the gold is exceedingly great, so far greater will be the change of our bodies and senses, much greater than we can now conceive. If grace makes Christians differ so much from what they were, that they could say to their companions, "I am not the person I was," how much more will glory make us different! We may then say much more, "This is not the body I had, and these are not the senses I had. But because we have no other name for them let us call them senses, call them eyes and ears, seeing and hearing: but conceive of the difference this way: that as much as a spiritual body, above the sun in glory, exceeds these frail, noisome, diseased lumps of flesh or dirt that now we carry about us, so far shall our senses of seeing and hearing exceed those we now possess: for the change of the senses must be conceived in proportion to the change of the body. And, doubtless, as God expands our senses and enlarges our capacities, so will God advance the happiness of those senses, and fill up all that capacity with himself.

And certainly the body would not be raised up and continued, if it could not share the glory. As it has shared in the obedience and sufferings, so it shall also share in the blessedness; and as Christ bought the whole of our humanity, so shall the whole partake of the everlasting benefits of the purchase.

The same difference must be allowed for the tongue. For though, perhaps, what we now call the tongue, the voice, the language, shall not then exist, yet, with this unimaginable change, it may continue. Certain it is, it shall be the everlasting work of those blessed saints, to stand before the throne of God and the Lamb, and to praise God for ever and ever. As their eyes and hearts shall be filled with God's knowledge, with God's glory, and with God's love, so shall their mouths be filled with God's praises. Go on, therefore, O saints, while you are on earth, in that divine duty. Learn, O learn, that saint-beseeming work, for in the mouths of God's saints God's praise is lovely. Pray, but still praise: hear and read, but still praise: praise God in the presence of God's people, for it will be your eternal work.

Oh, what then would I not either perform or part with to enjoy a clear and true apprehension of the most true God! How noble a faculty of the soul is the understanding! It can encompass the earth; it can measure the sun, moon, stars, and heaven; it can foretell each eclipse to a minute many years before: yes, but this is the top of all its excellency, it can know God who is infinite, who made all these, a little here, and more, and much more hereafter.

And if this were all, what a high favor that God will give us permission to love him; that he will allow himself to be embraced by the same arms that have embraced lust and sin before him! But this is not all; he returns love for love, yes, a thousand times more. As perfect as we shall be, we cannot reach his measure of love. Christian, you will be then brimful of love; yet love as much as you can, you will be ten thousand times more beloved. Do you think you can outlove God? What, love more than love itself? Were the arms of the Son of God open upon the cross, and an open passage made to his heart by the spear, and will not arms and heart be open to you in glory? Did God begin to love before you loved, and will not God continue now? Did God love you, an enemy, you a sinner, you who even loathed yourself, and own you when you disdained yourself; and will God not now immeasurably love you a child, you a perfect saint, you who returns some love for love? You were accustomed to question God's love; doubt of it then if you can.

Praise will be your eternal work.

DECEMBER 19

A reading from The Face of the Deep *by Christina Rossetti. on the text: "When the Lamb opened the seventh seal, there was silence in heaven for about half an hour." Revelation 8:1*

There seems to be a sense in which heaven waits on earth; in which (if I dare say so) God waits on us. Thus heaven now keeps silence as a prelude to earthly events, portents, vicissitudes. Yet this celestial silence need not convey to us (I conjecture) any notion of interruption in the day and night harmony of worship before the throne, any more than time interrupts eternity. For because we dare not think of God who "inhabits eternity" as changing to a habitation of time, we perceive that time and eternity co-exist, are simultaneous: if, that is, they are not instead different aspects of one and the same continuity.

If from the songs of heaven we learn to sing and make melody to the Lord with both voice and understanding, equally from the silence of heaven we may learn something. While heaven kept silence it appears that it may have been looking or preparing to look earthwards. And of old David declared: "I will keep my mouth with a bridle, while the wicked is before me. I was dumb with silence, I held my peace, even from good" (Psalm 39:2). Thus from angels above and from a saint below, I may study that meekness of righteous indignation, that discretion of holy zeal, which brings not railing accusations nor risks doing harm even by good words.

Silence seems unnatural, incongruous, in heaven. On this occasion and remotely we may surmise it to be a result of the Fall, for when earth first saw the light in panoply of beauty, the morning stars sang together and all the sons of God shouted for joy: sinless earth, for sinless it then seems to have been whether or not inhabited, called forth instead of silencing an outburst of celestial music.

I think one may view this "silence" as a figure of suspense. Reversing which proposition, I perceive that a Christian's suspense ought to present a figure of that silence. And if so, suspense should sustain my heart in heavenly peace even while fluttering over some spot of earth; and should become my method of worship, when other modes fail me; and should be adopted by my free will, whenever by God's will it befalls me; and should not hinder heaven from appearing heaven to me, or divorce me from fellowship with angels, or make me speak unadvisedly with my lips. Faithful, hopeful, loving suspense would be rich in evidence of things not seen and not heard; and would neither lag nor hurry, but would contentedly maintain silence during its imposed "half hour." A shorter time? no, on pain of rashness: a longer time? no, on pain of sullenness.

"About half an hour." Not finally, not for long. "Our God comes and does not keep silence, before him is a devouring fire, and a mighty tempest all around him. He calls to the heavens above and to the earth, that he may judge his people. . . . The heavens declare his righteousness"(Psalm 50:3–6).

The half moon shows a face of plaintive sweetness
    Ready and poised to wax or wane;
A fire of pale desire in incompleteness,
    Tending to pleasure or to pain:—
Lo, while we gaze she rolleth on in fleetness
    To perfect loss or perfect gain.

Half bitterness we know, we know half sweetness;
    This world is all on wax, on wane:
When shall completeness round time's incompleteness
    Fulfilling joy, fulfilling pain?—
Lo, while we ask, life rolleth on in fleetness
    To finished loss or finished gain.

Contentedly maintain silence.

DECEMBER 20

A reading from The Third Century *by Thomas Traherne.*

This sense that God is so great in goodness, and we so great in glory, as to be God's children and so rich as to live in communion with God, and so individually united to God that God is in us, and we in God, will make us do all our duties not only with incomparable joy, but courage also. It will fill us with zeal and fidelity, and make us to overflow with praises, for which one cause alone the knowledge of it ought infinitely to be esteemed, for to be ignorant of this is to sit in Darkness and to be a Child of Darkness: it makes us to be without God in the world, exceeding weak, timorous and feeble, comfortless and barren, dead and unfruitful, lukewarm, indifferent, speechless, unfaithful. To which I may add that it makes us uncertain, for so glorious is the face of God and true religion, that it is impossible to see it except in transcendent splendor. Nor can we know that God is, till we see God infinite in goodness. Nothing therefore will make us certain of God's being but God's glory.

To enjoy communion with God is to abide with God in the fruition of God's divine and eternal glory, in all God's attributes, in all God's thoughts, in all God's creatures; in God's eternity, infinity, almighty power, and sovereignty. In all those works which from all eternity God wrought, as the generation of the Son, the proceeding of the Holy Ghost, the eternal union and communion of the Blessed Trinity, the counsels of God's bosom, the attainment of the end of all God's endeavors wherein we shall see ourselves exalted and beloved from all eternity. We are to enjoy communion with God in the creation of the world, in the government of angels, in the redemption of mankind, in the dispensations of God's providence in the incarnation of God's Son, in his passion, resurrection, and ascension, in his shedding abroad the Holy Spirit, in his government of the church, in his judgment of the world, in the punishment of his enemies, in the rewarding of his friends, in eternal glory. All these therefore particularly ought to be near us, and to be esteemed by us as our riches, being those delectable things that adorn the house of God, which is eternity; and those living fountains, from whence we suck forth the streams of joy that everlastingly overflow to refresh our souls.

Eternity is a mysterious absence of times and ages: an endless length of ages always present, and for ever perfect. For as there is an immovable space wherein all finite spaces are enclosed, and all motions carried on and performed: so is there an immovable duration that contains and measures all moving durations. Without the first the last could not be; no more than finite places, and bodies moving without infinite space, all ages being but successions correspondent to those parts of that eternity wherein they abide, and filling no more of it than ages can do. Whether they are commensurate with it or no, is difficult to determine. But the infinite, immovable duration is eternity, the place and duration of all things, even of infinite space, itself: the cause and end, the author and beautifier, the life and perfection of all.

We are beloved from all eternity.

DECEMBER 21
A reading from The Spirit of Prayer *by William Law.*

No one can fail of the benefit of Christ's salvation, but through an unwillingness to have it. But if you would know how this great work, this birth of Christ, is to be effected in you, then let this joyful truth be told you: that this great work is already begun in every one of us. For this Holy Jesus that is to be formed in you, that is to be the Savior and new life of your soul, that is, to raise you out of the darkness of death into the light of life, and give you power to become a child of God, is already within you living, stirring, calling, knocking at the door of your heart and wanting nothing but your own faith and good will, to have as real a birth and form in you as he had in the Virgin Mary. For the Eternal Word, or Son of God, did not first begin to be the Savior of the world when he was born in Bethlehem of Judaea, but that Word which became human in the Virgin Mary did, from the beginning of the world, enter as a Word of Life, a Seed of Salvation into the first father of mankind, was inspoken into him as an ingrafted Word under the name and character of Bruiser of the Serpent's head. So it is that Christ said to his disciples "The kingdom of God is within you," that is, the divine nature is within you which was given to your first father, to the light of his life, and from him, rising up in the life of every son of Adam. So also the Holy Jesus is said to be the "Light which enlightens everyone who comes into the world." Not as he was born at Bethlehem, not as he had a human form on earth; in these respects he could not be said to have been the light of everyone who comes into the world, but as he was that Eternal Word by which all things were created, which was the Life and Light of all things and which had as a second Creator entered again into fallen humanity, as a Bruiser of the Serpent. In this respect it was truly said of our Lord when on earth that "He was that Light that enlightens everyone who comes into the world." For he was really and truly all this, as he was the Immanuel, the "God with us" given to Adam, and in him to all his offspring.

See here the beginning and glorious extent of the Catholic Church of Christ: it takes in all the world. It is God's unlimited universal mercy to all mankind, and every human creature as sure as he or she was born of Adam, has a birth of the Bruiser of the Serpent within, and so is infallibly in covenant with God through Jesus Christ. So also it is that the Holy Jesus is appointed to be Judge of all the world; it is because all mankind, all nations and languages have in him and through him been put into covenant with God and made capable of resisting the evil of their fallen nature.

Poor sinner, consider the treasure you have within yourself: the Savior of the world, the eternal Word of God lies hidden in you, as a spark of the divine nature which is to overcome sin and death and hell within you, and generate the life of heaven again in your soul. Turn to your heart, and your heart will find its Savior, its God within itself. You see, hear, and feel nothing of God because you seek for God abroad with your outward eyes, you seek for God in books, in controversies, in the church and outward exercises, but there you will not find God till you have first found God in your heart. Seek for God in your heart, and you will never seek in vain.

Seek for God in your heart.

Mary's Girlhood

This is the blessed Mary, pre-elect
God's virgin. Gone is a great while, and she
Dwelt young in Nazareth of Galilee.
Unto God's will she brought devout respect
Profound simplicity of intellect.
And supreme patience. From her mother's knee
Faithful and hopeful; wise in charity;
Strong in grave peace; in pity circumspect.

So held she through her girlhood; as it were
An angel-watered lily, that near God
Grows and is quiet. Till, one dawn at home
She woke in her white bed, and had no fear
At all—yet wept till sunshine, and felt awed:
Because the fullness of the time was come.

Gabriel Charles Dante Rossetti

DECEMBER 22

A reading from Religious Studies *by Harriet Beecher Stowe.*

There was one woman whom the voice of a divine messenger, straight from heaven, pronounced highly favored. In what did this favor consist?

Of noble birth, of even royal lineage, she had fallen into poverty and obscurity. The great, brilliant, living world of her day knew her as the rushing equipages and palatial mansions of our great cities know the daughters of poor mechanics in rural towns.

There was plenty of splendor, and rank, and fashion in Jerusalem then. Herod the Great was a man of cultivation and letters, and beautified the temple with all sorts of architectural embellishments; and there were high priests, and Levites, and a great religious aristocracy circling about its precincts, all of whom, if they thought of any woman as highly favored of heaven, would have been likely to think of somebody quite other than the simple country girl of Nazareth. Such an one as she was not in all their thoughts. Yet she was *the* highly favored woman of the world; the crowned queen of women; the One whose lot—above that of all that have lived woman's life, before or since—was blessed.

The views adopted in the Roman Church with respect to this one Woman of women have tended to deprive the rest of the world of a great source of comfort and edification by reason of the opposite extreme to which Protestant reaction has naturally gone.

John Knox was once taken on board a ship manned, as he says, by Popish sailors, who gave into his hand an image of the Virgin Mary and wanted to compel him to kiss it. Stout John tossed it overboard, saying, "Let our Lady now save herself; she is light enough, let her learn to swim." To have honored the Virgin Mary, even in thought, was shrunk from by the Protestants of those times as an approach to idolatry. An image or a picture of her in a Puritan house would have been considered an approach to the sin of Achan. Truth has always had the fate of the shuttlecock between the conflicting battledores of controversy.

This is no goddess crowned with stars, but something nobler, purer, fairer, more appreciable—the One highly favored and blessed among women.

The happiness of Mary's lot was peculiar to womanhood. It lay mostly in the sphere of family affection. Mary had in this respect a lot whose blessedness was above every other mother. She had as her child the loveliest character that ever unfolded through childhood and youth to manhood. He was entirely her own. She had a security in possessing him such as is not accorded to other mothers. She knew that the child she adored was not to die till he had reached man's estate—she had no fear that accident, or sickness, or any of those threatening causes which give sad hours to so many other mothers, would come between him and her.

Neither was she called to separate from him. The record shows that he was with his parents until their journey to Jerusalem, when he was twelve years old; and then, after his brief absence of three days when he was left behind, and found in the temple disputing with the doctors, we are told that "he went down to Nazareth and was subject unto them."

These words are all that cover eighteen years of the purest happiness ever given to mortal woman. To love, to adore, to possess the beloved object in perfect security, guarded by a divine promise—this blessedness was given to but one woman of all the human race. That peaceful home in Nazareth, overlooked by all the great, gay world, how many happy hours it had! Day succeeded day, weeks went to months, and months into years, and this is all the record: "Jesus increased in wisdom and in stature, and in favor with God and man."

She was the crowned queen of women.

DECEMBER 23

A reading from Religious Studies *by Harriet Beecher Stowe.*

If we should embody our idea of the Son with whom Mary lived in secure intimacy for thirty years, we should call him LOVE itself. He was not merely lovely, but he was love. He had a warming, creative power as to love. He gave birth to new conceptions of love; to a fervor, a devotion, a tenderness, of which before the human soul scarcely knew its own capacity.

The blessedness of Mary was that she was the one human being who had the right of ownership and intimate oneness with the Beloved. For thirty years Jesus had only the task of living an average, quiet, ordinary human life. He was a humble artisan, peacefully working daily for the support of his mother. He was called from her by no public duty; he was hers alone. When he began his public career, he transcended these limits. Then he declared that every soul that heard the will of God, and did it, should be to him as his mother—a declaration at which all Christians should veil their faces in awe and gratitude.

There was one woman of all women to whom it was given to know him perfectly, entirely, intimately—to whom his nature was knit in the closest possible union and identity. He was bone of her bone and flesh of her flesh—his life grew out of her immortal nature. We are led to see in our Lord a peculiarity as to the manner of his birth which made him more purely sympathetic with his mother than any other son of woman. He had no mortal father. All that was human in him was her nature; it was the union of the divine nature with the nature of a pure woman. Hence there was in Jesus more of the pure feminine element than in any other man. It was the feminine element exalted and taken in union with divinity. Robertson has a very interesting sermon on this point, showing how the existence of this feminine element in the character of Jesus supplies all that want in the human heart to which it has been said the worship of the Virgin Mother was adapted. Christ, through his intimate relationship with this one highly favored among women, had the knowledge of all that the heart of man or woman can seek for its needs. There is in her whole character a singular poise and calmness. When the angel of the Annunciation appeared to her she was not overcome by the presence of a spiritual being as Daniel was, who records that "he fell on his face and there was no strength in him." Mary, in calm and firm simplicity, looks the angel in the face, and ponders what the wonderful announcement may mean. When she finds that it really does mean that she, a poor lonely maiden, is the chosen woman of all the human race—the gainer of the crown of which every Jewish woman had dreamed for ages—she is still calm. She does not sink under the honor, she is not confused or overcome, but answers with gentle submission, "Here am I, the servant of the Lord; let it be with me according to your word."

Yet the words of the Magnificat show a keen sense of the honor and favor done her. She exults in it with an innocent heartiness of simplicity. "He has looked with favor on the lowliness of his servant. Surely, from now on all generations will call me blessed."

Enough is recorded of her to make her forever dear to all Christian hearts. That Mary is now with Jesus, that there is an intimacy and sympathy between her soul and his such as belong to no other created being, seems certain. Nor should we suffer anything to prevent that just love and veneration which will enable us to call her Blessed, and to look forward to meeting her in heaven as one of the brightest joys of that glorious world.

Call her blessed.

DECEMBER 24

A reading from a sermon for Christmas Eve by John Keble on the text: "the dawn from on high will break upon us, to give light to those who sit in darkness and in the shadow of death, to guide our feet into the way of peace." St. Luke 1:78–79

Now whether there was fault in these Bethlehemites finding no room for them in the inn, or whether it was what we call an accident, the warning, my friends, to you and to me, and to all within reach of the gospel, is just the same. We know beforehand what those Bethlehemites could not know, who he is that will come among us tomorrow; and who is even now saying to us, "Prepare me a lodging in your hearts." We are as persons within a house, who have heard one speaking at their door, late, it may be, in the evening, who know well enough who it must be that is knocking. If people under such circumstances do not arise and open the door, it can only be because they care very little about him who is waiting to come in; or because they have used him ill, and are afraid and ashamed to look him in the face.

Hear his own words while he is willing to wait outside the door of your heart, not bearing to go away, and leave you to your ruin. "Listen!" he says, "I am standing at the door, knocking; if you hear my voice and open the door, I will come in to you and eat with you, and you with me" (Rev. 3:20). And he has given up all for you, he has "poured out his soul unto death"; he is even now marked with the five cruel wounds he received in your behalf upon the cross; and what is it he asks from you? Why does he court a lodging in such a place as you know your heart to be? For no good at all to himself, but for the greatest possible good to you. For he is seeking, my friends, to have himself spiritually born in you. He once promised and who may gainsay him? "Whoever does the will of my Father in heaven is my brother and sister and mother" (Matt. 12:50).

If you do his Father's will, he accounts you his own mother; that is, he condescends to be spiritually born within you; and to have his own image and likeness gradually growing in your heart and life, until it comes to maturity. And even if you have once been his, and have swerved from him, he does not give you up. St. Paul so yearned after some who had transgressed and forgotten his teaching, that he wrote to them, "My little children, for whom I am again in the pain of childbirth until Christ is formed in you" (Gal. 4:19). He loved them as his very own, with the love not only of a father, but of a mother. His love of them was so great, his fear of their going wrong so urgent, his sense of the importance of the moment so over-whelming, that he could compare it to nothing but the travail-pangs of a mother. If St. Paul, an under-shepherd, so felt for his own flock, how much more the Savior and God of St. Paul, who by his Spirit poured into the apostle's heart all the love he ever did, or at any time could bear to a sinner? O depend upon it, however sinful you may have been, he longs very exceedingly to be spiritually born again in you. He is still knocking at your door, where you have kept him waiting, it may be, many years. Indeed, before now, you have perhaps rudely bidden him be gone. The least, surely, that any of us can do is to welcome with a glad and thankful heart him who so lovingly comes again to visit us. To be rude and sullen to a visitor is a churlish, hateful thing, and so considered even among the heathen; the common feeling of all mankind rises up against one who can behave so. What then, if you be found hereafter, in the hearing of all humanity and all angels, guilty of shutting out your best and only benefactor, seeking in so many ways to come to you for your good?

Christmas is now a joyful word to almost all of us, because of the earthly comforts and refreshments which the time commonly brings with it; but it will be a fearful word by and by, if in looking back to past years, we shall have to confess that we have kept so many of Christ's birthdays, with hardly one serious thought of Christ, that we have enjoyed the carols, the holidays, the good cheer, the merry meetings, but never applied ourselves to repenting of our sins, nor to serious thoughts of how we may learn to love him, who has so freely and wonderfully loved us.

Christ is still knocking at your door.

Christmas Eve

Christmas has a darkness
   Brighter than the blazing noon,
Christmas has a chillness
   Warmer than the heat of June,
Christmas has a beauty
   Lovelier than the world can show:
For Christmas brings us Jesus,
   Brought for us so low.

Earth strike up your music,
   Birds that sing and bells that ring;
Heaven has answering music
   For all angels soon to sing:
Earth put on your whitest
   Bridal robe of spotless snow:
For Christmas brings us Jesus,
   Brought for us so low.

Christina Rossetti

DECEMBER 25

A reading from LI Sermons *by Mark Frank on the text: "And she gave birth to her firstborn son and wrapped him in bands of cloth, and laid him in a manger, because there was no place for them in the inn." St. Luke 2:7*

I shall not need to tell you who this "she," or who this "him." The day rises with it in its wings. This day wrote it with the first ray of the morning sun upon the posts of the world. The angels sang it in their choirs, the morning stars together in their courses. The Virgin Mother, the Eternal Son. The most blessed among women, the fairest of the sons of men. The woman clothed with the sun; the sun compassed with a woman. She the gate of heaven: he the King of Glory that came forth. She the mother of the everlasting God: he God without a mother; God blessed for evermore. Great persons as ever met upon a day.

Yet as great as the persons, and as great as the day, the lesson of them both is to be little, to think and make little of ourselves; seeing the infinite greatness in this day become so little, Eternity a child, the rays of glory wrapped in rags, heaven crowded into the corner of a stable, and he that is everywhere in want of a room.

I may at other times have spoken great and glorious things, both of the persons and the day: but I am determined today to know nothing but Jesus Christ in rags, but Jesus Christ in a manger. And I hope I shall have your company along; your thoughts will be my thoughts, and my thoughts yours, and both Christ's; all upon his humility and our own. This is our firstborn, which we are this day to bring forth, for it is a day of bringing forth; this we are to wrap up in our memories, this to lay up in our hearts; this the blessed mother, this the blessed babe; this the condition and place and time we find them in, the taxing time, the beast's manger, the swaddling clothes—all this day preach to us.

What though there be no room in the inn, though the world will not entertain him? The devout soul will find a place to lay him in, though it have nothing of its own but rags, a poor ragged righteousness, yet the best it has it will lay him in, and though it have nothing but a manger, a poor straight narrow soul, not the cleanest either to lodge him in; yet such as it is, he shall command it, his lying there will cleanse it, and his righteousness piece together our rags.

What though there be no room for him in the inn? I hope there is room in our houses for him. It is Christmas time, and let us keep open house for him; let his rags be our raiment, his manger our Christmas cheer, his manger our Christmas great chamber, hall, dining room. We must dress with him and feed with him and lodge with him at this feast. He is now ready by and by to give himself to eat; you may see him wrapped in the swaddling clothes of his blessed sacrament; you may behold him laid upon the altar as in his manger. Do but make room for him and we shall bring him forth, and you shall look upon him and handle him and feed upon him; if we bring only the rags of a rent and torn and broken and contrite heart, the white linen clothes of good intentions and honest affections to swathe him in, wrap him up fast, and lay him close to our souls and bosoms.

It is a day of mysteries; it is a mysterious business we are about: Christ wrapped up, Christ in the sacrament, Christ in a mystery. Let us be content to let it go, believe, admire, and adore it. It is sufficient that we know Christ's swaddling clothes: his righteousness will keep us warmer than all our winter garments, his rags hold out more storms than our thickest clothes; let us put them on. His manger feeds us better than all the Asian delicacies, all the dainties of the world; let us feed our souls upon him. The stable is dark, but there is the light of the world to enlighten it. The smell of the beasts, our sins, are perfumed and taken away with the sweet odors of holy pardon and forgiveness. The noise of the ox and ass are stilled with the music of the heavenly host; the noise of our sins with the promises of the gospel brought to us this day.

Let us not then think much to take him wrapped up, that is in a mystery, without examining how and which way we are to receive him. Let us be content with him in his rags, in his humblest and lowest condition; it is the way he comes to us today. Let us ourselves wrap him and lay him up in the best place we can find for him, though the best we have will be little better than a manger.

Make room for him.

DECEMBER 26—St. Stephen

A reading from a sermon by Frederick Denison Maurice for St. Stephen's Day on the text: "Look, I see the heavens opened and the Son of Man standing at the right hand of God." Acts 7:56

When Stephen said, "Look, I see the heavens opened and the Son of Man standing at the right hand of God" (Acts 7:56), that truth which he had been proclaiming presented itself to him just as actually as any visible thing presents itself to the eye. It was not a doctrine of the incarnation that he acknowledged in that hour—a mere doctrine would have stood him in little stead. It was a Person who stood before him, a person on whom he might call, in whom he might trust. He was sure it was life and substance he was in contact with. It was a Son of Man, the fellow worker and fellow-sufferer with every human being; One who had broken down the distinction while he was on earth between publican and Pharisee; One who would break down the distinction, older and more sacred still, between Jew and Gentile. Was it not an opening of heaven which disclosed such a union of humanity with divinity? Did not that opening of heaven foretell a shaking of all religions—of all politics on earth—which stood on some other foundation than this; which either severed humanity from God or tried to fashion a God out of the human notions?

Yes! This was the witness, the distinctive Christian witness; that which it was worthwhile to die for, that which it was possible to die for. An immense majority might vote it ridiculous, but its truth or falsehood depended on no majority. Stephen could cast it forth on the earth to perish, if it was an opinion of his or anyone else or of any age.

Would it, then, have surprised him to hear that this truth might have to be vindicated in after days as it was in his days against consistories of religious doctors substituting their dead systems for a living Creator and Father; denying that God had really been made known to us or that there is really a way from us to God. Would he not count it inevitable that any society which had learned to regard truth as a mere dominant opinion, to be enforced as other opinions are enforced, would lose its connection with him who is the Truth, would become hard-hearted and inhuman, therefore un-Christian, and would need to be reminded, even by those who do not bear the name of Christ, what he is and what he came into the world to do?

St. Stephen's witness is the witness which the church of God is to bear upon earth. The true martyr bears that witness and no other.

But this would be a very impractical conclusion if it did not lead each of us to ask, "How may I, in my place and calling, bear witness to this Son of Man, if I indeed believe that there is a Son of Man and that he has revealed God to us and that he stands at the right hand of God?" I think, my friends, that no people can less escape that inquiry than we, the members of the Anglican Church. By every act and service from Advent to Trinity, by the language of our confessions, prayers, thanksgivings, by our creeds and sacraments, we solemnly avow Sunday after Sunday, day after day, our belief that there is truly a Son of Man, one in all things with us, who has justified and glorified our human race at the right hand of God. I doubt not that any who are raised up to testify on behalf of the truth which enabled Stephen to fall quietly asleep with a prayer for his country and for those who were stoning him will always find these creeds mighty aids and comforts. Still less can I doubt that the Bible in its plain history, stripped of all refinements, will be to them, as the early part of it was to St. Stephen, the chief strengthener of their faith, the great weapon against all artificial, notional, exclusive religion.

Judging according to human calculation there never was a time when such witnesses were more demanded or were less likely to appear. But we are not to judge according to human calculations. This is God's own cause, and God will take care of it. In places of which we know nothing, by process of education which we cannot guess, God may have been preparing these witnesses. In the very year that is coming they may appear in our lands or in lands which we suppose in our vanity need reformation more. Whenever or wherever they arise they will speak with power to the hearts of those who need the Son of Man. They will be sure, even when their own vision is weakest, that the heavens will one day be opened and that the Son of Man will be revealed to the whole universe at his Father's right hand.

How may I bear witness?

DECEMBER 27—St. John the Evangelist

A reading from a sermon by Frederick Denison Maurice on the text: "I tell you, many will come from east and west and will eat with Abraham and Isaac and Jacob in the kingdom of heaven, while the heirs of the kingdom will be thrown into the outer darkness, where there will be weeping and gnashing of teeth." St. Matthew 8:11, 12

This is St. John's Day. We have read from the Apocalypse words that are beautiful commemorations of it. They tell us how the Apostle himself wished his contemporaries to think of him. He had borne witness to the Word of God and to the testimony of Jesus Christ. He was their brother and companion in tribulation, and in the kingdom and patience of Jesus Christ.

But "the heirs of the kingdom," so the text goes, "will be thrown into the outer darkness, where there will be weeping and gnashing of teeth." I would beseech you to observe the language of our Lord, and not to change it for any phrases of ours. We certainly cannot make it clearer or fuller than he has made it. He speaks of darkness: St. John tells us why: "*This*," he says, "is the judgment, that the light has come into the world, and people loved darkness rather than light because their deeds were evil" (John. 3:19).

The Light of the World shines forth upon mankind. Those who should hail it and spread it through the world are scared by it; fly from it, hate it. Either they must establish their reign of darkness, or the Light must prove itself stronger than they are. It does prove itself stronger, therefore they are left to the darkness which they have chosen. It is *outer* darkness; it lies outside of God's kingdom, outside of humanity. God's order has banished it.

We feel and know that the signs of a kingdom of God are among us; every Christmas Day testifies that it has been brought near to us; that we are living, moving, having our being in the midst of it. It is with us, close to the heart of each one of us. The Word of God is preaching to us of it there. That Word of God converts every record of the past into a message for the present. Stephen looks at us as he did at the Jewish Sanhedrin, with the face of an angel. For us he witnesses, for us he dies. John is our brother and companion in tribulation, and in the kingdom and patience of Jesus Christ. The Innocents mingle with the children who are born and die before our eyes. All testify of a kingdom undefiled and eternal, into which we may enter, the treasures of which are for us all. And about us all are powers of darkness which would persuade us that there is no kingdom of light which would draw us beyond its circle. They tell us that the world which speaks to eye, ear, taste, is the only real world. We believe them, and the beauty of that world vanishes; what looked—what was—full of life and motion and freedom, becomes dull and hopeless. We do not abandon our religion because we become sensualists; but our religion becomes one of terror and hatred; a system of devices to escape from God, to cause the Holy One to cease from us. Oh, friends, that Christendom, that our land, may never so dally with these powers of darkness as at last to be brought into that outer darkness! Oh that we may never gnash with our teeth because God's Word speaks to our consciences of good things that were ours, and that we would not have! Oh that the warnings of this year—that the deliverances of this year—may be received as God's own loving entreaties to us, not to cast ourselves into this torment! But whether we receive them as such or not, multitudes will come from the east and the west, from north and the south—and sit down in the kingdom of Abraham, Isaac, and Jacob. As sure as day rises out of night—as year succeeds year—will the one who stood before John in the Isle of Patmos: be revealed to the eye of every creature. As surely as the voice of any earthly friend is speaking to us warning or comfort, is he saying, "Behold! I come quickly, and my reward is with me, to give to all as their work shall be."

Signs of a kingdom of God are among us.

DECEMBER 28—Holy Innocents
A reading from The Irrational Season *by Madeleine L'Engle.*

Holy Innocents' Day is a stumbling block for me. This is a festival? this remembering the slaughter of all those babies under two years of age whose only wrong was to have been born at a time when three Wise Men came out of the East to worship a great King; and Herod, in panic lest his earthly power be taken away from him by this unknown infant potentate, ordered the execution of all the children who might grow up to dethrone him.

Jesus grew up to heal and preach at the expense of all those little ones, and I have sometimes wondered if his loving gentleness with small children may not have had something to do with this incredible price. And it causes me to ask painful questions about the love of God. St. Catherine of Siena said, "Nails were not enough to hold God-and-man nailed and fastened on the cross, had not love kept him there." What kind of love was that? More like folly. All the disciples except John had abandoned him. His mother was there and a few women as usual, and a gaping mob, also as usual, and some jeering soldiers. That's all. The cross represented the failure of his earthly mission. God came to the world and the world didn't want him and threw him out by crucifying him like a common criminal. God—God the Father—loved the world he had created so much that he sent his only son—that spoken Word who called forth something from nothing, galaxies from chaos—he sent him to dwell in human flesh, to accept all earthly limitations, to confine himself in mortal time; and when this beloved son begged in agony that he might be spared the cross, what did the Father do? No thunderbolts, no lightning flash. Silence was the answer to the prayer. No was the answer. And Jesus of Nazareth died in agony on the cross; the love of God echoing back into the silence of God.

That is love? How can we understand it? Do we even want it? I sometimes get very angry at God, and I do not feel guilty about it, because the anger is an affirmation of faith. You cannot get angry at someone who is not there. So the raging is for me a necessary step toward accepting that God's way of loving is more real than man's, that this irrational, seemingly unsuccessful love is what it's all about, is what created the galaxies, is what keeps the stars in their courses, is what gives all life value and meaning.

But what kind of meaning? It's not a meaning that makes any sense in a world geared to success and self-fulfillment.

Remember the children in the school bus hit by a train? Remember the Vietnamese orphans dying in a flaming plane? What about all the holy innocents throughout time?

God has a strange way of loving; it is not our way, but I find evidence in my own experience that it is better than our way, and that it leads to fuller life, and to extraordinary joy.

Because I am a writer I live by symbol, and because I was born in the Western World my symbolism is largely Judaeo-Christian, and I find it valid, and the symbol which gives me most strength is that of bread and wine. Through the darkness of my uncomprehending, through my pain and weakness, only thus may I try to become open to God's love as I move to the altar to receive the body and blood, and accept with friend and neighbor, foe and stranger, the tangible assurance that this love is real. It is real, but it is not like our love.

If the dark prophets who infuriated the people of the Establishment in their own day have anything to say to me today, it is through their constant emphasizing that God is so free of his own creation that he can transform us in our pain into a community of people who are able to be free of the very establishments which are formed in his name. For these establishments inevitably begin to institutionalize God's love and then he teaches us (put my tears in your bottle) what love really is—not our love, not what we want God's love to be, but God's love.

This love is not like our love.

DECEMBER 29

A reading from a sermon by Lancelot Andrewes on the text: "But the angel said to them, 'Do not be afraid; for see—I am bringing you good news of great joy for all the people: to you is born this day in the city of David a Savior, who is the Messiah, the Lord.'" St. Luke 2:10–11

I know not why it is that when we hear of saving or of a Savior, our mind is carried to the saving of our skin, and other saving we think not of. But there is another life not to be forgotten, and the dangers and destruction there are more to be feared than those here, and it would be well sometimes to remember that. Besides our skin and flesh we have a soul, and that is our better part by far, and also has need of a Savior. It has a destruction out of which and a destroyer from which it should be saved, and this should be thought of. Indeed our chief thought and care should be for that: how to escape the destruction to come, to which our sins will certainly bring us.

Sin it is which will destroy us all, and there is no person on earth who has so much need of a Savior as does a sinner. There is nothing so dangerous, so deadly to us, as the sin in our hearts; nothing from which we have so much need to be saved, whatever account we make of it. From it comes all the evil of this life and of the life to come. In comparison of that last, the evil here is not worth speaking of. Above all then we need a Savior for our souls, and from our sins, and from the everlasting destruction which sin will bring on us in the other life, which is not far from us, not even from the one who thinks it furthest away.

Then if it is good tidings to hear of a Savior when it is only a matter of the loss of earth, or of this life here, what is it when it comes to the loss of heaven, to the danger of hell, when our soul is at the stake and the welfare or destruction of it for ever? One who could save our souls from that destroyer—would not the birth of such a one be good news? Is not such a Savior worth listening to? Is he not? Is it then because we lack that sense of our souls and the dangers of them that we have of our bodies, nor that fear of our spiritual enemies, nor that awareness of the eternal torments of that place, and how near we are to it, nothing being between us and it but this poor puff of breath which is in our nostrils. Our bodies are living and sensitive, our spirit is dead and dull. We lack the feeling of our sins that we have of our sickness. If we had, we would hear this news with greater cheerfulness and hold this day of the birth of such a Savior with joy indeed. We cannot conceive it yet. This destruction is not near enough to affect us. But in the end, when the destroyer shall come and we shall want a Savior, we shall plainly understand and value this benefit and the joy of it as we ought, and find there is no joy on earth like the joy of a Savior.

There is no joy like the joy of a Savior.

A reading from the sermon "Christmas Haste" by Charles Henry Brent on the text: "They came with haste, and found both Mary and Joseph, and the babe lying in the manger." St. Luke 2:16

The shepherd lads animate the Christmas story with their racing feet, as a generation later two running disciples the Easter narrative, illustrating the demeanor of every earnest character in the presence of a new phase of truth. Vehement desire binds wings to the feet. Need rouses desire; responsibility challenges capacity. Few of us have heard our desire sing its full song; few have plumbed the true depth of our own capacity.

So they made haste—those shepherd folk—because the parched lips of high desire were within reach of cooling streams, because the restless wings of human searching were but an arrow's flight from home, because the in-coming tide of God's love had caught human capacity in its resistless embrace to carry it to its life goal. The shepherds left their sheep in the care of the merry stars, and hastened to Bethlehem to reach the core of things, to press within the veil. They went not with the blackness of the night veiling their eyes, but in the radiance of a vision. Forgetful of self they looked with eager intentness into the depths of revelation. Past cot and fold they sped, past home and crowded inn, until they reached the palace gate. Within, the smoking torch, the lowing beast, the silent, watching man, the happy mother, the Babe. And what is it they see? In the embrace of the manger-bed a Babe. There is nothing to distract them from his human babyhood—no lace-fringed trappings, no dainty coverlet, no golden spoon. Coarse swathing-bands enfold him, the kindly straw is his cushion, a mother's breast his only comfort, he who was above nature left no room for doubt that he was a part of nature.

The shepherds went back to their duty, and forever after their sheepfold was an angels' choir, a court of heaven, as they sat under the stars with eyes that dared not slumber, lest while they slept some new vision of the King in his beauty should spring out of the night.

As one looks over the Christian world there is such unappeased hunger among honest, earnest men and women as to give the beholder the same sense of pain as would rack him were he to see his own brother dying of malnutrition or starvation. Why do we dally? The angels have sung to us and pointed to the banquet table. But our feet are laggard and our pulse beats slow. We fear for the welfare of our sheep, we say. We shall lose foothold among men. We shall endanger our intellectual consistency. Or perhaps it is that we do not like the appearance of a manger or the surroundings of a stable. We are bidden to the church—the church that is so full of errancy and imperfection and failure. But the shepherds did not hesitate to leave their sheep. Too exclusive attention to our task keeps God from having a share in it. We need the relief that comes from godly carelessness; or, to put it in less paradoxical language, we are suffering from the strain of constant calculation and anxiety. Those who learn to take rest in God, after a while become able to do their work in God, and spend their odd moments painting pictures of heaven on the walls of their workshop.

It is true, indeed, that Christ is to be found only in a manger. The shepherds were told so, but they did not respond that, because he was not in a palace, they would remain with their browsing flocks under the clean stars. The most loyal adherent of the church does not contend that it is ideal, only that Christ is there. It is strange that he should be willing to make it the chief sphere of his manifestation on earth, but it is one of the strange things that are true, like mirrored beauty in a muddy pool, the chaste pearl within the rude oyster-shell.

Modern life is fine in many of its aspects; it is diligent in its labors, honest in its investigations, courageous in its enterprises. But it lacks one thing needful. It is too reasoned, and not sufficiently spiced with the recklessness of those whose idealism is a controlling force that sends them to the Bethlehem manger with the racing feet of Christmas haste.

Why do we dally?

DECEMBER 31

A reading from a New Year's Eve sermon by John Mason Neale on the text: "a time to be born, and a time to die." Ecclesiastes 3:2

I think the text suits the occasion. It speaks to you of death: there is a time to be born and a time to die; it speaks of Christmas: there is a time to be born; it speaks of the birth of the new, and the departure of the old year: there is a time to die. And now I want you to notice this. Solomon is here reckoning up the different things for which in the course of these lives of ours, there is a season. And the two first and the two last answer in a certain way to each other: a time to be born and a time to die, a time of war and a time of peace. As much as to say: the time of being born is the time when, like some valiant general, we ought to go forth to war, a hard war, a long war, a war in which we are beset with all manner of enemies, a war in which we wrestle "against principalities, against powers, against the rulers of the darkness of this world, against spiritual wickedness in high places"; the time to die is the time when, like the same general, after many losses, many dangers, it may be many defeats, we nevertheless return home with victory, and enter into everlasting peace.

Think of that birth, when it was indeed time for the world that the King of kings and the Lord of lords should be born: when the fullness of that time was come which the Father had foreordained from all eternity: the time, as an old writer says, of new redemption, ancient restoration, of eternal felicity. That was the time in which the Child, then born to us, the Son, then given to us, went out to war: not to one battle and then an end: not to one year's fighting, and then the peace, but to a wearisome struggle of thirty-three years and more, a struggle against all manner of enemies, a struggle with all sorts of difficulties. We rightly begin the year with the first sufferings of our Lord, because by means, and only by means of those sufferings, we hope to attain to that blessed country where they reckon not their time by days and years. This then, is the time in which our Lord thought it meet to be born. But we no sooner remember that, than we remember also that it is the time in which he ordained that his first martyr should die. Christ now descended, that Stephen might now ascend: Christ came down into the manger of Bethlehem, that Stephen might go up into the palace of heaven: Christ was wrapped in swaddling clothes, that Stephen might be endued with the robe of immortality: for Christ there was no room in the inn, that for Stephen there might be one of the many mansions in the eternal city: Christ entered amid the songs of the angels, that Stephen might depart amid the blasphemies of those who stoned him. Not an ill time then (is it?) to die, that in which St. Stephen saw heaven opened, and the Son of Man standing on the right hand of God, that in which too, the Holy Innocents set forth the praise of the Lord, not by their words but by their blood.

And now look at the two years: the poor old worn-out year, that had seen so much sorrow and suffering and sickness and sin, and was gathered to its fathers at midnight, and the new year, so full of hope and vigor and expectation, as yet. There has been a time to die for the one; there is a time to be born for the other.

I cannot tell—which of us can tell?—whether it may or may not please God that this year on which we have now entered shall be one of more rest and quietness to us than the last. It ought not to matter. In whatever situation it pleases God to place us, there we know that we are given the opportunity, if we will, of working out our own salvation. Yet, I trust that God may make our enemies to be at peace with us. We have all of us enemies enough in our own hearts, I am quite sure, to take up all our time and all our thoughts, without their being thus distracted. For this I have prayed earnestly, that the Prince of Peace, at whose birth, when he came into the world, peace was sung by the angels, and who when he was going out of the world, bequeathed peace to his apostles, may give peace in our time: peace, not from strife within ourselves, for that, while we live in the flesh, we always must have, but peace from earthly enemies here, and, in the world to come, that perfect peace which can never—no not for one moment—be broken, because Jerusalem is the vision of peace.

Pray for peace.

JANUARY 1—The Circumcision (Holy Name)

A reading from a sermon by Isaac Williams on the text: "After eight days had passed, it was time to circumcise the child; and he was called Jesus, the name given by the angel before he was conceived in the womb." St. Luke 2:21

The day of the circumcision tells us that to follow Christ we must be in a manner dead to this world while we are in it; that we must not seek to do our own will or follow our own pleasure, if we would learn to love God now and be with God hereafter. If this seems a hard saying, let us ask the world what it has to promise. It will tell us, as on this day, that if we fix our hearts upon any thing on earth, it will very soon depart from us, or we shall depart from it and leave it behind. A consideration of the fleetness of our days which a new year brings to our minds, tells us that the time of our stay is so uncertain, and so short at the longest, that it really matters very little what we have and what we have not, what we may suffer or what we may enjoy, if only we may be admitted at last into the blessed kingdom of God's rest.

The gospel indeed calls us to mortification; but what is this? It only calls on us to give up that which will soon give us up if we do not; to give it up in order that we may obtain something infinitely better, to give up earthly hopes and treasures for heavenly, that we may not lose both. To be ever looking up as the faithful Abraham did, feeling ourselves but as strangers and pilgrims in a land that is not our own; that with a more free heart we may walk with God. Nature says, "I die daily"; the grave is being dug for me. Grace also says the same, "I die daily"; but adds, "I die that I may live"; for a mansion is being prepared for me which is above, The world will tell us on this day that neither riches, nor honor, nor friends, nor learning will make us one year younger, or delay our departure to that place from which there is no return. Does this sound melancholy? The gospel tells us on this day that we have no business with such desires and disappointments as the world brings, for we have been bound to renounce them long ago, that we may have our hearts and treasure elsewhere.

So far as we look for satisfaction in things temporal, another year passing over our heads must bring with it many melancholy reflections. But if any are steadfastly purposed to follow Christ with the aid of his Blessed Spirit, and in all things to deny their own will in order to be conformed to the will of God, to them every passing year may afford encouragement and satisfaction, as it brings nearer to an end that state in which they must die daily, in order that they may live eternally.

Such is the true circumcision of the spirit by which Christians become new creatures. All things are become new to them, and as they grow older in this world, there is a new world opening upon them, new heavens and a new earth, in which righteousness dwells.

Every year that has borne us onward in our course as it goes by is indeed a call for more active exertion, for more steadfastly setting our face toward the heavenly Jerusalem, to be more earnest and constant than ever in the duties of religion; to forget the things that are behind, and to press forward more eagerly to that which is before: the prize of the high calling in Christ Jesus.

Press forward eagerly.

JANUARY 2

A reading from a sermon by John Newton on the text: "In that region there were shepherds living in the fields, keeping watch over their flock by night. Then an angel of the Lord stood before them, and the glory of the Lord shone around them . . . And suddenly there was with the angel a multitude of the heavenly host, praising God and saying, 'Glory to God in the highest heaven, and on earth peace among those whom he favors!'" St. Luke 2:8, 13–14

The gratification of the great, the wealthy, and the gay was chiefly consulted in the late exhibitions in Westminster Abbey. But notwithstanding the expense of the preparations, and the splendid appearance of the auditory, I may take it for granted that the shepherds who were honored with the first information of the birth of the Messiah enjoyed at free cost a much more sublime and delightful entertainment. How poor and trivial is the most studied magnificence and brilliancy of an earthly court compared with that effulgence of glory which surrounds the shepherds! The performers of this oratorio, if I may be allowed the expression, were a multitude of the heavenly host. And though I do not suppose that the angel delivered the message in the cadence which is called *recitative*, I have no doubt that the chorus was a *song*, sweetly melodious as from blessed voices, a song which the redeemed and the angels of the Lord are still singing before the throne. A new song. A song which will always be new. We are made acquainted with the subject, indeed with the very words of this song. May our hearts be suitably affected by the consideration of them today!

The melody and harmony of heaven are far above our conceptions. The music of that happy land has no dependence upon the vibrations of the air or the admirable structure of the human ear. But we have reason to believe that there is, in the world of light and love, something analogous to what we call music, though different in kind and vastly superior in effect to any strains that can be produced by the most exquisite voices and instruments upon earth, as we readily judge the glory of the angel to be unspeakably more excellent both in kind and degree than anything that is deemed glorious among mortals.

Assuredly this song of the heavenly host is not the language of our hearts by nature. We once sought our pleasure and happiness in a very different way. We were indifferent to the glory of God and strangers to God's peace. And some of us are still blind to the excellencies of the gospel and deaf to its gracious invitation. But we must not expect to sing with the great company of the redeemed hereafter before the throne of glory unless we learn and love their song while we are here. Those who attain to the inheritance of the saints in light are first made meet for it in the present life and in this way. They believe the testimony of the Scripture respecting their own guilt, unworthiness, and helplessness; then they receive the record which God has given of the Son. They renounce all "confidence in the flesh" (Phil. 3:3), they rejoice in Christ Jesus, and from his fullness they derive grace to worship God in the Spirit. A sense of their obligations to the Savior disposes them to praise him now as they can, and they rejoice in hope of seeing him before long as he is, and that then they shall praise him as they ought. For heaven itself, as described in the Word of God, could not be a state of happiness to us unless we are like-minded with the apostle to "regard everything as loss because of the surpassing value of knowing Christ Jesus my Lord" (Phil. 3:8).

Some of us are still blind.

JANUARY 3

A reading from the sermon "The Showing Forth of Christ" by John Donne.

The whole life of Christ was a continual passion; others die martyrs but Christ was born a martyr. He found a Golgotha (where he was crucified) even in Bethlehem, where he was born; for to his tenderness then the straws were almost as sharp as the thorns after and the manger as uneasy at first as his cross at last. His birth and his death were but one continual act, and his Christmas Day and his Good Friday are but the evening and the morning of one and the same day. And as even his birth is his death, so every action and passage that manifests Christ to us is his birth.

Every manifestation of Christ to the world, to the church, to a particular soul, is an Ephiphany, a Christmas Day. Now there is nowhere a more evident manifestation of Christ than in that which induced this text: "Master, now you are dismissing your servant in peace . . . " It had been revealed to Simeon (whose words these are) that he should see Christ before he died. And actually, and really, substantially, essentially, bodily, presentially, personally, he does see him; so it is Simeon's Christmas Day.

Contenting ourselves with so much therein as was according to his word, and not inquiring farther than God had been pleased to reveal; and having reflected all these several beams upon every worthy receiver of the sacrament, the whole choir of such worthy receivers may join with Simeon in this antiphon, "Master, now you are dismissing your servant in peace."

Neither can we at any time be fitter to make and obtain this wish than when our eyes have seen his salvation in the sacrament. At least make this an argument of your having been worthy receivers thereof, that you are in an evenness, in an indifferency, in an equanimity whether you die this night or no. Who can fear the darkness of death that has had the light of this world and of the next too? Who can fear death this night that has had the Lord of life in his hand today? Origen asks, "When will you dare to go out of this world, if you dare not go now, when Christ Jesus has taken you by the hand to lead you out?" This then is truly to depart in peace by the gospel of peace to the God of peace. If you did depart from that Table in peace you can depart from this world in peace. And the peace of that Table is to come to it with a contented mind and with an enjoying of those temporal blessings which you have, without usurping upon others, without murmuring at God; and to be at that Table in the peace of the church, without the spirit of contradiction or inquisition, without uncharitableness toward others, and then to come from that Table with a bosom peace in your own conscience, in that seal of your reconciliation, in that sacrament; that so, riding at that anchor and in that calm, whether God enlarge your voyage by enlarging your life, or put you into the harbor by the breath, by the breathlessness of death, either way, east or west, you may depart in peace, according to his word, that is, as he shall be pleased to manifest his pleasure upon you.

This is truly peace.

JANUARY 4

A reading from a sermon by Phillips Brooks on the text: "And the Word was made flesh, and dwelt among us." St. John 1:14

There is one group which no one who thinks of Christmas Day forgets: "There were shepherds abiding in the field, keeping watch over their flock by night." How familiar and how full of rich association these old words have grown! Try to think what their story must mean, what contribution it makes to the symphony of meaning in which all these attendants on the birth of Christ unite. Remember what is told us. They heard a song of angels, a voice from heaven telling them that a Savior was born in Bethlehem, and that glory had come to God and peace had come to earth. Then they can only say to one another, "Let us go to Bethlehem and see this strange thing." Then they come and find Christ, and then they go abroad to tell others about him. That is all. There is a certain dumb, blind movement about all they do, yet with a certain simple, eager straightforwardness about it. They sing no psalm like Mary. They do not follow the star nor go to Herod like the wise men. They simply hear a voice from heaven telling them that there is a Savior and where he is, and they say, "Let us go there." And they do go there and they do find him.

I am sure that I need not tell you what an eternal element in Christian life they represent. Always there will be those who will be exalted with the thought of the incarnation, upon all whose life and occupations it will cast a glorifying light. Always there will be those who out of much unrest and anarchy will seem to come into a rich and conscious peace as they submit themselves to Christ's kingship. But such experiences will always seem too subtle for some souls. Always there will be many whose whole experience will be merely this: that, hungry, needy, empty, wanting a Savior, they just heard a voice from heaven telling them that the Savior whom they needed had come, and they just went to him and found him all they wanted, and then, like the poor shepherds, "made known abroad" to others all that had come to them. No doubt in their experiences, simple as they seem, the whole richness of those others will really be included. But to the multitude of human souls Christ will be simply the Satisfier revealed from heaven, and they will turn to him almost as a creature shut up in the dark turns without thought, without plan or anticipation, to any corner of its darkness where a bright light suddenly shines.

Are there not moments in the Christian life of all of us when this alone is all our Christianity? We are told this and that about Jesus, this and that subtle thought about the mystery of his nature, this and that profound theory of the work by which he makes himself our redeeming King. We do not doubt and we do not deny. It is as if, when we were turning with full heart aching or sympathy to find our dearest friend, someone should stop us and tell us deep things about the philosophy of friendship, We do not doubt and we do not deny. It may be true. No doubt it is true. But all is overswept and drowned for the time by a blind, eager, passionate longing of the hearts that need Christ to get to them. People tell us why we need him. We cannot listen, but our heart is full of one consciousness: that we do need him. Our lips can shape only one question: "Where shall we find him?" Our wills are all absorbed in one strong resolution: "Let us go now to him."

It is good for us to think as richly and deeply of Christ as we can. It is good for us to analyze in patient meditation all that he is to us and all that we can be toward him. But oh, let us beware lest any subtlety of thought or depth of meditation ever deadens or dulls in us that first great, deep longing of the soul for him who is its only Savior. In deepest grief, in uttermost perplexity, often in great and overwhelming joy, always in conscious sin, that yearning, that unquestioning and passionate desire, asserts itself. It is as instinctive as the movement of the hurt child to its mother, or of the parched beast to the river. Always at the bottom of such strong experience what is stirred really is the sense of sin, and that none but the Jesus sent to take away our sins really can relieve. By his forgiveness, by himself given to us, he does forgive it, and then, while others call the wondrous Lord by partial names that utter some one side of his wondrousness, to us he has but one name—Savior. He is that and that alone, and all besides only as it is wrapped up in that.

It is a day of joy and charity. May God make you very rich in both by giving you abundantly the glory of the incarnation, the peace of Christ's kingship, and the grace of Christ's salvation.

He has but one name—Savior.

JANUARY 5

A reading from a sermon by Frederick Denison Maurice on the text: "And the Word became flesh and lived among us, and we have seen his glory, the glory as of a father's only son, full of grace and truth." St. John 1:14

Some will tell you that people are not as merry now on this day as they used to be. One says that this is a grievous thing, that we should try if we can to bring back the old times. Another says, "This cannot be, people are wiser now. They know that one day is no better than another; the thing is to be real Christians in our hearts." Another tells us "Christmas Day is forgotten, because that which Christmas Day speaks of does not signify so much as it once did. It was good for the people who lived a thousand years ago to believe such tales; but we have better and more solid things to care for." My friends, I will tell you what I believe is the truth about these notions, which different people will puzzle you with. To those who say, "Let us bring back the old times—let us be merry as we used to be," I would say, "Well! but we cannot be merry merely because we try to be so. We cannot be merry unless there is something to make us merry. If our hearts be glad we shall find ways to express our gladness, but we do not make our hearts glad by pretending that they are so, or by putting on the outward signs of jollity."

It may be, friends, that easy, comfortable people make less of Christmas Day than they once did. Perhaps they will presently make less of it than they do now. If the Bible be true, this was to be expected. For hear what Isaiah says, and St. Peter repeats the words, "The grass withers, the flower fades; but the word of our God will stand forever" (Isaiah 40:8). As if he had said, "All that has grown out of this root shall drop off in order that it may be seen how deeply the root itself is fixed in the soil." We do not keep Christmas in the bright, sunny time of the year, but now in the heart of winter, when everything is bare and dry. And our Lord himself is said to be "a root out of a dry ground," that, indeed, from which all the blossoms of hope and joy are to come, but which must first be owned in its own nakedness before they shall appear. If then, my friends, people have begun to fancy that their gladness has another root than this, it is good that for a time they should be left to try whether they can keep it alive by any efforts and skill of theirs. If

Christmas joy has been separated from Christ, it is no wonder and no dishonor to Christ that it should grow feeble and hollow. But Christmas is not dead because the mirth of those who have forgotten its meaning is dead. It is not dead for you, it is not dead for people who lie upon beds tormented with fevers, and dropsies, and cancers. It is not dead for the children in factories, and for the men who are working in mines, and for prisoners who never see the light of the sun. To all these the news: "The Word who was in the beginning with God and was God, in whom is life, and whose life is the light of all people, by whom all things were made, and without whom was not anything made that was made, became flesh and dwelt among us, entered into our poverty, and suffering, and death,"—is just as mighty and cheering news now as it was when St. Peter first declared it on the day of Pentecost. You want this truth, my friends, you cannot live or die without it. You have a right to it. By your baptism God has given you a portion in him who was made flesh; by your suffering he is inviting you to claim that portion, to understand that it is indeed for you Christ lived and died. You may live as if no such news as this had ever been proclaimed in the world, but it is not the less true that it has been proclaimed, and proclaimed for you. And blessed be God, this proclamation is not made merely through weak, mortal lips; that altar bears a more deep and amazing witness of it than it is possible for these words of mine to bear. There you may learn how real the union is which the living Word of God established with human flesh; how truly that flesh is given to be the life of the world. Christmas Day declares that he dwelt among us. To those who here eat his flesh and drink his blood, he promises that he will dwell in them, and that they shall dwell *in* him. This is the festival which makes us know, indeed, that we are members of one body; it binds together the life of Christ on earth with his life in heaven; it assures us that Christmas Day belongs not to time but to eternity.

You want this truth.

THE EPIPHANY—January 6

A reading from a sermon by Lancelot Andrewes on the text: "In the time of King Herod, after Jesus was born in Bethlehem of Judea, wise men from the East came to Jerusalem, asking, 'Where is the child who has been born king of the Jews? For we have seen his star at its rising, and have come to pay him homage.'" St. Matthew 2:1–2

Consider the time of their coming, the season of the year. It was no summer progress. A cold coming they had of it at this time of the year, just the worst time of the year to take a journey, and especially a long journey. The ways deep, the weather sharp, the days short, the sun farthest off, the very dead of winter.

And these difficulties they overcame: of a wearisome, irksome, troublesome, dangerous, unseasonable journey. And, for all this, they came, and came cheerfully and quickly, as it seems by the speed they made. "They saw" and "they came"; no sooner did they see than they set out. They took all these pains, made all this haste so they might be there to worship him with all the possible speed they could. They were sorry only that they could not be there soon enough, with the very first, to do it even this day, the day of his birth.

And we, what would we have done? Surely these men of the East will rise in judgment against us, and their faith against ours. With them it was simply, "we see" and "we come"; with us it would have been "we *will* come" at best. Our fashion is to see and see again before we stir a foot, especially if it be to the worship of Christ. Come on such a journey at such a time? No; but let us put it off to the spring of the year, till the days are longer, and the ways fairer, and the weather warmer, and it is better traveling to Christ. Our Epiphany would surely have fallen in Easter week at the soonest.

But then the distance, desolateness, tediousness, and the rest would be enough to mar our coming completely. It must first be no great way we must come; we love not that. The shepherds fared well but they came from nearby; we prefer them to the Magi. No, not like them either; for with us the nearer may be farther off. You know the proverb: "The nearer the church, the farther from God."

And it must be through no desert. If the way is rugged and uneven, if the weather is ill-disposed, if there is ever so little danger, it is enough to stay us. To Christ we cannot travel unless the weather and way and all are fair. If not, then there will be no journey, but we will sit still and see what happens. Indeed, all our religion is rather a seeing, a contemplation, than a motion or a stirring to do anything.

And when we do it, we must be allowed leisure: ever coming, never come. We love to make no very great haste. To other things perhaps, but not to worship. Why should we? Why talk of twelve days? If it is forty days hence, you shall be sure to find his mother and him; she cannot be "churched" until then, so what is the need of haste? The truth is we take him and his birth but slenderly. Best get us a new Christmas in September; we are not likely to come to Christ at this feast.

Consider their coming.

Author Biographies

Lancelot Andrewes (1555–1626)
The favorite preacher of James I, Lancelot Andrewes preached the Christmas sermon for the king every year between 1605 and 1624. His scholarship and linguistic ability live on in the King James Version of the Bible, of which he was a principal translator, and his piety, reflected in his *Private Prayers (Preces Privatae)*, has continued to influence Christians through the centuries.

Richard Baxter (1615–1691)
Although dissatisfied with many aspects of the Church of England, Baxter tried to ignore the differences between Presbyterian, Independent, and Anglican and to secure the cooperation of all in a common pastoral work. He joined the Parliamentary army for a while but disliked Cromwell's religious views and so became chaplain to a royalist regiment. With the Parliamentary victory, he went into retirement and wrote his classic work, *The Saints' Everlasting Rest*.

Richard Mieux Benson (1824–1915)
Vicar of Cowley, two miles from Oxford, Benson was inspired by a sermon of John Keble's to found the Society of St. John the Evangelist, known as the "Cowley Fathers," the oldest religious order for men in the Anglican Communion. He continued as superior of the order until 1890 and was widely known for his preaching and other writings.

John Bowring (1792–1872)
Although John Bowring's early education was directed toward a career as a merchant, his interest in political and social reform led him instead to become an influential member of Parliament. At the

age of fifty-eight, he was appointed consul in Canton and then appointed governor of Hong Kong. An accomplished linguist, Bowring wrote several volumes of devotional poetry. His experience in the Far East is thought to underlie the dialogue between the traveler and watchman in his best known hymn, "Watchman, tell us of the night."

Charles Henry Brent (1862–1929)
One of the most influential Christians of the twentieth century, Charles Henry Brent was born in Canada, served an urban congregation in Boston, and then was made the first missionary bishop of the Philippines. Brent convened an international conference on the opium trade, served as Senior Chaplain for the American armed forces in World War I, became bishop of Western New York, and convened the first International Conference on Faith and Order in 1927.

Phillips Brooks (1835–1893)
Perhaps the greatest preacher in the history of American Christianity, Phillips Brooks was Rector of Trinity Church, Boston, and later Bishop of Massachusetts but he is probably best known as the author of the Christmas hymn, "O little town of Bethlehem."

Richard William Church (1815–1890)
An associate of Pusey, Keble, and Newman in the early days of the Oxford Movement, R. W. Church founded the *Guardian* as a paper to espouse the principles of the movement. He became Dean of St. Paul's Cathedral, London, in 1871, and held that position until his death in 1890. Although he helped edit the writings of the early church fathers and wrote biographies of St. Anselm, Spenser, and Bacon, he is best known for his balanced and judicious history of the Oxford Movement.

John Donne (1573–1631)
Although his secular poetry continues to be read, Donne is probably best known today for his "Holy Sonnets" and the eloquent sermons he preached during his ten years as Dean of St. Paul's Cathedral, London.

Austin Farrer (1904–1968)

The son of a Baptist minister, Austin Farrer was ordained in the Church of England and served as Dean of Magdalene College, Oxford, and Warden of Keble College while building a reputation as an eloquent preacher, writer, and poet.

Mark Frank (1612–1664)

Master of Pembroke Hall, Cambridge, and Archdeacon of St. Albans, Mark Frank was a scholar and preacher who lost his positions during the English Civil War because of his royalist sympathies but was reinstated when the monarchy was restored. He was a friend of Nicholas Ferrar and influenced in his preaching style by Lancelot Andrewes.

John Keble (1792–1866)

After a brief career at Oxford, John Keble resigned in 1823 to assist his father in a country parish in the Cotswolds. There he composed the poems which were published in 1827 under the title *The Christian Year*, which led in turn to his appointment as Professor of Poetry at Oxford. With Newman and Pusey, Keble became one of the leaders of the Oxford Movement and worked with Pusey to keep that movement within the Church of England when Newman defected to Rome.

Thomas Ken (1637–1711)

A man of strong principle, Ken refused to let King Charles come into his house with his mistress, was sent to the tower for refusing to sign James II's Declaration of Indulgence, and refused also to take the oath of allegiance to William and Mary when they replaced James II. As a result, Ken was deprived of his position as Bishop of Bath and Wells; he lived the remainder of his life in retirement. He is best known today for his hymns and, in particular, the familiar doxology, "Praise God from whom all blessings flow."

Hugh Latimer (1485–1555)

Appointed Bishop of Winchester in 1535, Latimer was confined to the tower for his reforming beliefs in 1546 but released when Edward VI became king. Arrested again on the accession of Mary,

Latimer was burned at the stake with Nicholas Ridley in 1555. His preaching was noted for its homely style and ready wit. As the son of a yeoman farmer, he knew how to speak to ordinary people in language they understood.

William Law (1686–1781)
One of the most important writers in the history of English Christianity, William Law's *Serious Call to a Devout and Holy Life* was a significant influence on John Wesley and laid the foundation for the evangelical revival in the eighteenth century.

Madeleine L'Engle (1918–   )
Born in New York City, Madeleine L'Engle is probably best known for her books for children such as *A Wrinkle in Time*, many of which explore the interface between science and religion. Her writing includes theological meditations such as *The Irrational Season*, novels such as *A Severed Wasp*, and books drawn from her own life experience such as *The Summer of the Great-grandmother* and *Two-Part Invention*.

Frederick Denison Maurice (1805–1872)
The son of a Unitarian minister, Frederick Denison Maurice came by degrees into the Church of England and was ordained in 1834. He joined with others to found a Christian Socialist movement and founded a Working Men's College in London to promote his socialist ideals. Although he wrote a number of biblical studies, his most enduring work is *The Kingdom of Christ: Hints to a Quaker concerning the Principle, Constitution, and Ordinances of the Catholic Church.*

John Mason Neale (1818–1866)
A scholar and translator, John Mason Neale served for most of his ministry as Warden of Sackville College, East Grinstead, where he instituted an order of nursing sisters and worked to set forward the ideals of the Oxford Movement. Among the best known of his many hymns and translations are "All glory, laud, and honor," "Come, ye faithful, raise the strain," and "Christ is made the sure foundation."

John Newton (1725–1807)

The son of a shipmaster, Newton was involved in the slave trade before coming under the influence of George Whitefield and studying for the ministry. He was ordained in 1764 and served from 1780 until his death as Rector of St. Mary, Woolnoth, in London. He is best known as the author of such hymns as "Glorious things of thee are spoken" and "Amazing grace."

Edward Bouverie Pusey (1800–1882)

Ordained a priest in 1828, Pusey was appointed Regius Professor of Hebrew at Oxford and held that position the rest of his life. With Keble and Newman, Pusey led the Oxford Movement through its early days but became the primary leader after Newman's defection to Rome.

Christina Georgina Rossetti (1830–1894)

Christina Rossetti is probably best known for her Christmas carol, "In the bleak mid-winter," but she wrote many other hymns, poems, and books, including a devotional commentary on the Book of Revelation.

Gabriel Charles Dante Rossetti (1828–1882)

A painter and poet, in 1848 Rossetti founded the Pre-Raphaelite Brotherhood with Holman Hunt and others. Rossetti was deeply influenced by the poetry of Dante. Of all his poems, the best known is probably "The Blessed Damozel" with its Dantesque view of heaven.

Elizabeth Rowe (1674–1737)

In a time when very few women were able to write for publication, Elizabeth Rowe was the author of a number of books of poetry and devotional writings. Born in Ilchester, Somersetshire, in 1674, to "a gentleman of good family," she began to write poetry at the age of twelve and had her first collection of poems published ten years later at the urging of friends such as Thomas Ken, the Bishop of Bath. She wrote a paraphrase of the thirty-eighth chapter of Job at the bishop's request and a three-volume life of Joseph. Married briefly to Thomas Rowe, who died at the age of twenty-eight, she died in 1736 or 1737.

Dorothy L. Sayers (1893–1957)

A student of medieval literature, Dorothy L. Sayers was one of the first women to graduate from Oxford. Ten years later, she began the series of Lord Peter Wimsey detective stories that won a wide readership. Later in life she turned to theology, writing plays and books, and to a translation of *Dante's Divine Comedy*, which was not quite finished when she died.

Harriet Beecher Stowe (1811–1896)

Best known as the author of *Uncle Tom's Cabin* and, as legend has it, for being referred to by Abraham Lincoln as "the little lady that started this war," Harriet Beecher Stowe was the daughter, sister, and mother of such eminent Congregational clergy as Lyman Beecher and Henry Ward Beecher. Nonetheless, by 1866 she had become a member of Trinity Church, Hartford, Connecticut. She encouraged her daughters to become Episcopalians, and worked to help build an Episcopal church near her winter home in Florida.

Jeremy Taylor (1613–1673)

A distinguished scholar and theologian, Jeremy Taylor was deprived of his living during the Commonwealth period but was made Bishop of Down and Connor when the monarchy was restored. His *Holy Living* and *Holy Dying* had an enormous influence on English Christians for generations after his death.

Thomas Traherne (1637–1674)

Thomas Traherne was born in Hereford, the son of a carpenter, and was ordained a priest in 1660 after taking his B.A. degree from Oxford. Until his death, he served a small parish near Hereford and the works for which he is now known, especially the *Centuries of Meditations*, were not published until the early twentieth century. He is now recognized as one of the great mystical writers of the Anglican tradition.

Isaac Williams (1802–1865)

A poet and theologian, Isaac Williams was educated at Oxford and drawn into the Tractarian Movement through the influence of John Keble. Controversy over his writing cost him election to the chair of poetry, and as a result he withdrew from Oxford to spend his life in retirement, writing sermons and poetry.

Bibliography

Andrewes, Lancelot. *Sermons on the Nativity*. Grand Rapids, Mich.: Baker Book House, 1955, pp. 73–74, 253–54.

Baxter, Richard. "The Saints' Everlasting Rest." In *Anglicanism*. Edited by Paul Elmore More and Frank Leslie Cross. New York: Macmillan, 1957, pp. 328–31.

R. M. Benson. *The Religious Vocation*. London: A. R. Mowbray, 1939, pp. 282, 56–57, 61, 65–66.

Bowring, John. *The Hymnal 1982*. New York: Church Publishing Incorporated, 1985, no. 640.

Brent, Charles Henry. *A sermon preached at St. Stephen's Church, Boston, on Christmas Day, 1904.*

———. *The Mount of Vision*. London and Bombay: Longmans, Green and Co., 1904, pp. 120–25.

Brooks, Phillips. *Selected Sermons*. Edited by William Scarlett. New York: E. P. Dutton, 1950, pp. 371–77.

———. *Sermons for the Principal Festivals and Fasts of the Christian Year*. Edited by John Cotton Brooks. New York: E. P. Dutton, 1895, pp. 93–96.

Church, R. W. *Advent Sermons*. London: Macmillan, 1886, pp. 88–94.

Donne, John. *The Sermons of John Donne*. Vol. 10. Edited by George R. Potter and Evelyn Simpson. Los Angeles: University of California Press, 1953–1962, pp. 229–48.

Farrer, Austin. *The Crown of the Year*. Westminster: Dacre Press, 1952, pp. 7–8, 10.

Frank, Mark. *LI Sermons*. London: Andrew Clark, publisher for John Martyn, Henry Brome, and Richard Chiswell, 1672, pp. 36–38, 77–91

Keble, John. *Sermons for the Christian Year*. Vols. I and II. London: Walter Smith, 1885, pp. 296–99.

Ken, Thomas. *The Works of the Rt. Rev. Learned and Pious Thomas Ken, D.D.* Vol. IV. London: John Wyat, 1721, pp. 52–56.

Latimer, Hugh, *Sermons and Remains of Hugh Latimer, Sometime Bishop of Worcester*. Edited for the Parker Society by the Rev. George Elwes Corrie. Cambridge: University Press, 1845.

Law, William. *The Pocket William Law*. London: Latimer House, 1950, pp. 128–31.

L'Engle, Madeleine. *The Irrational Season*. New York: Seabury Press, New York, 1977, pp. 2–4.

Maurice, F. D. *The Ground and Object of Hope for Mankind, Four Sermons Preached before the University of Cambridge in November 1867*. Cambridge: Macmillan, 1868, pp. 95–99.

———. *Sermons*. Vols. III, 69–82; and V, 69–75. London: John F. Taylor, undated.

———. in *The English Sermon*. Vol. III. Edited by Robert Nye. Cheadle, Cheshire, Great Britain: Carcanet Press, 1976, pp. 208–11.

Neale, John Mason. "Appointed Time." In *Sackville College Sermons*. Project Canterbury [cited 15 July 2001]. Available from *justus. Anglican.org/resources/pc/neale*.

Newton, John. *The Works of the Rev. John Newton*. Vol. III. New York: Williams and Williams, 1810, pp.115–16, 126.

Pusey, Edward Bouverie. *Everlasting Punishment: A Sermon Preached before the University in the Cathedral Church of Christ, in Oxford*. London: J. and F. H. Rivington, 1865, pp. 14–21.

———. *Parochial Sermons*. Vol. I. Oxford: John Henry and James Parker, 1864, pp. 116–119, 419–35.

Rossetti, Christina G. *The Face of the Deep: A Devotional Commentary on The Apocalypse*. London: Society for Promoting Christian Knowledge, 1911, pp. 241–42.

———. *Verses by Christina Rossetti*. London: Society for Promoting Christian Knowledge, 1904, p. 54.

Rossetti, Gabriel Charles Dante, "Mary's Girlhood," *The World's Great Religious Poetry*. New York: Macmillan, 1926.

Rowe, Elizabeth, "Devout Exercises of the Heart." In *The Easter Spirit*. Edited by Robert Van de Weyer and Pat Saunders. London: Darton, Longman, and Todd, 1990, pp. 76–77.

Sayers, Dorothy L. *Introductory Papers on Dante*. London: Methuen & Co. and New York: Barnes & Noble, Inc., 1969, pp. 66–67.

Stowe, Harriet Beecher. *Religious Studies: Sketches and Poems*. Boston: Houghton Mifflin, 1896, pp. 30–40.

Taylor, Jeremy. *The Rule and Exercises of Holy Dying*. Philadelphia: Thomas Wardle, 1846, pp. 13–16.

Traherne, Thomas. *Traherne: Poems, Centuries, and Three Thanksgivings*. Edited by Anne Ridler. London: Oxford University Press, 1966, pp. 314–15, 370.

Williams, Isaac. *A Series of Sermons on the Epistle and Gospel for Each Sunday in the Year and the Holy Days of the Church*. Vol. 1. London: Rivingtons, 1855, pp. 78–82.